POSITIVELY SINGLE

POSITIVELY SINGLE

Harold Ivan Smith

VICTOR BOOKS
A DIVISION OF SCRIPTURE PRESS PUBLICATIONS INC.
USA CANADA ENGLAND

Unless otherwise noted, Scripture quotations are from the *Holy Bible, New International Version,* © 1973, 1978, 1984, International Bible Society. Used by permission of Zondervan Bible Publishers. Other quotations are from the *King James Version* (KJV); *The Living Bible* (TLB), © 1971, Tyndale House Publishers, Wheaton, IL 60189; and the *New American Standard Bible* (NASB), © the Lockman Foundation 1960, 1962, 1963, 1968, 1971, 1972, 1973, 1975, 1977. Used by permission.

Recommended Dewey Decimal Classification: 248
Suggested Subject Heading: SINGLE ADULTS

Library of Congress Catalog Card Number: 85-63315
ISBN: 0-89693-154-4

CONTENTS

DEDICATION

To James A. Brown, Ph.D.
my doctoral advisor at Rice

SPECIAL THANKS

To Patti Reynolds and Karen DeSollar
for editorial assistance

WHAT DOES IT MEAN TO BE AN ADULT? I

Leafing through a magazine recently I was captivated by an ad sponsored by the Girls Clubs of America. In crayoned child's print, I read:

> When I grow up a rich man will fall in love with me and marry me and take care of me.

When I grow up is a common theme among children. Parents frequently deny a child's request with a "when you grow up, *then*" statement. They demand of teenagers, "When are you ever going to grow up?"

What does it mean to be a grown-up? An adult? Adults pay higher prices for concerts, ball games, and dinners. Movie ratings suggest "adult language and/or situations." In many large cities you can find "adult" bookstores. Luxury apartment complexes post *adults only* signs. And of course there are "adult strength" formulas for headaches, iron-poor blood, and constipation.

In the past there were four tests for adulthood:

- old enough to marry without parental permission
- old enough to purchase alcoholic beverages
- old enough to vote
- old enough to serve in the military

But not everyone agrees on the criteria. In most states as of January 1, 1984 you have to be either sixteen or eighteen to drive. However, in Louisiana, Maine, Montana, and New Mexico you can get a driver's license at age fifteen. Those states have never been known for their jammed interstates, anyway. In some states teens can get a juvenile license at age fifteen with parental permission (Idaho, Kansas, Nevada, Oregon, North Dakota, and Nebraska).

Marriage has been perceived as another adult rite. Yet in Alabama, Kansas, New Hampshire, Rhode Island, South Carolina, Texas, and Utah you can get married at age fourteen with parental consent. Without the parents' consent, in forty-nine states the minimum age is eighteen.

Adulthood carries cultural expectations. Two decades ago, many men by age twenty-one had a wife, two or three children, a steady job, and a mortgage. Yet in twenty years a major change has developed as the mean age at first marriage has increased to 25.4 years for males and 22.8 years for females.[1]

So what does it mean to be an adult?

Webster defines *adult* as "fully developed and mature" or grown-up. But how does one know he or she is "fully developed and mature"? I've met some eighteen-year-olds who seemed mature and some fifty-eight-year-olds who seemed immature. Is it possible that one can be physically mature and "fully developed" and yet be underdeveloped in the spiritual or emotional arenas?

Robert Havinghurst, a developmental psychologist, formulated what he called "the developmental tasks of adulthood." Supposedly, on every young adult's agenda were eight responsibilities:

1. Selecting a mate.
2. Learning to live with a mate.
3. Starting a family.
4. Rearing children.
5. Managing a home.
6. Getting started in an occupation.
7. Taking on civic responsibility.
8. Finding a congenial social group.[2]

But what about the millions of single adults for whom

items one through five are inappropriate? What about those young adults who focus primarily on items six and eight?

Consider Havinghurst's agenda for middle adulthood:

1. Assisting teenage children to become responsible and happy adults.
2. Achieving adult social and civic responsibility.
3. Reaching and maintaining satisfactory performance in one's career.
4. Developing adult leisure activities.
5. Relating to one's spouse as a person.
6. Accepting and adjusting to physiological changes.
7. Adjusting to aging parents.[3]

How do these agenda items affect you?

WHERE DOES FAITH FIT INTO THE AGENDA?

Can you be an adult and fully mature without spiritual maturity as well? Doesn't faith touch or influence our priorities and goals? Augustine said, "We are restless until we find our rest in Thee."

We have all heard a friend or colleague who has scurried up the career ladder moan, "Is this all there is?" Or he's discovered that at the top of the ladder is yet another ladder. The question *Is there life after death?* has been replaced by *Is there life* during *life?*

Certainly, a strong biblically-rooted faith enables and encourages us, whatever our age or stage, to face our agendas—especially those that involve threat, risk, or change. Paul wrote that the church's task was "to prepare God's people for works of service, so that the body of Christ may be built up *until we all* reach unity in the faith and in the knowledge of the Son of God and become mature, attaining to the whole measure of the fullness found in Christ" (Eph. 4:12-13).

In essence, Paul offers his own working definition of adulthood: "attaining the full measure of perfection found in Christ." The fully matured single adult will then "no longer be tossed back and forth by the waves, and blown here and there by every wind of teaching." Our agenda for spiritual adulthood is to "*in all things* grow up into Him who is the Head, that is, Christ" (vv. 14-15). Our goal is maturity in *all* dimensions of our lives, not just the spiritual.

Many human potential experts and pop psychologists offer easy paths to personal and spiritual growth—and we crave easy, painless solutions. But personal growth does not come without a struggle and a great deal of hard work. No wonder Paul exclaimed, "See to it that *no one* takes you captive through hollow and deceptive philosophy, which depends on human tradition and the basic principles of this world rather than on Christ. For in Christ all the fullness of the Deity lives in bodily form, and you have been given fullness in Christ" (Col. 2:8-10).

David Duncombe in *The Shape of the Christian Life* identified these building blocks in personal development:

- a freeing sense of security
- self-expression without fear
- accurate perception of the world and other people
- adequate response to varied human situations[4]

In other words, the mature Christian adult can face tomorrow's surprises, disappointments, and heartaches. Not because of college degrees or certificates from training programs or seminars attended, but because of Christ.

WHERE DOES TEAMWORK FIT IN?

Lawrence Crabb and Dan Allender are helpful in explaining the difference between a goal and a desire. A goal is "a purpose to which a person is unalterably committed." The person "assumes unconditional responsibility for that goal, and it can be achieved if he is willing to work at it."[5] The human potentialists and possibility thinkers say "Amen to that!"

However, Crabb and Allender define *desire* as a purpose "that cannot be obtained without the cooperation of others."[6] Clearly, adulthood (spiritual/physical) is part of God's design for us. But adulthood cannot be obtained without the active help of others. We are not called to be lone rangers (Gen. 2:18).

God gave Adam a "helpmeet" or helper. Our society insists that everyone should pair up. It's been that way since the unloading of the ark. But are we to flounder in limbo until our tardy Prince or Princess Charming shows up? Or can these solo days be a time of maturing to become all that God wants us to be?

I was fascinated by the front-page story of a recent *Dallas Observer*. The headline read:

How Does It Feel to Be Single and Over 30?

The answer stunned me: "It feels . . . *awful*."[7] While the article was written from a secular perspective, many Christian unmarrieds would probably agree. And that's tragic!

WHERE DOES GROWTH FIT IN?

Colleges and universities, to keep their accreditations, periodically have to go through "self-studies." This process determines their strengths and weaknesses so that the institution is not depending on past reputation but on present academic realities. Alfred Armand Montapert has formulated some personal "self-study" questions. Take time to consider your answer to each of these:

- Am I doing the things that make me happy?
- Are my thoughts of noble character?
- How can I simplify my life?
- What are my talents?
- Does my work satisfy my soul?
- Am I giving value to my existence?
- How can I improve my life?[8]

To these I would add:

- Am I seeking FIRST the kingdom of God?
- Is Jesus my Lord?

Whatever keeps you from enjoying the abundant life Jesus promised probably keeps you from being fully matured too. Hopefully, when you've finished reading this book you will be more committed to attaining that full measure of perfection to be found in Christ. To positive singlehood. Alan Jones in *Exploring Spiritual Direction* raised three significant questions:

- Do I really believe that my life comes to me as a gift and that there is in me a terrific thing?
- Am I, in the middle of my own struggles, daring enough to ask for help, seek guidance, cultivate friendships?
- Am I sincere in wanting to respond to my longings for God and for growth, especially when I know and fear the revolutionary changes that may be involved?[9]

In this book we will formulate a creative agenda for adulthood, an agenda for "taking stock." An agenda is only a list or plan of things to be considered or accomplished. An agenda, in a spiritual sense, is to do that which will cause the Master to say, "Well done, good and faithful servant!" (Matt. 25:21)

An agenda will have its share of whiteouts, U-turns, right turns, and surprises. In the first of my doctoral work, my ambition was to become a college president. Several fellow students have now reached that goal. But en route, my agenda changed. I'd now rather be a writer.

Sometimes the change agents may be unpleasant. Few of our lives unfold without detours. But as the songwriter noted,

> Whatever my lot, Thou hast taught me to say,
> It is well, it is well with my soul![10]

What about your adulthood? Can you say that "it is well"?

In the *Book of Common Prayer* this prayer challenged me:

> Thank You for setting us at tasks which demand our best efforts, and for leading us to accomplishments which satisfy and delight us. Thank You for those disappointments and failures that lead us to acknowledge our dependence on You alone.[11]

On some of our agendas no doubt there will be tragedies. A headline in the *Kansas City Times* recently proclaimed:

A Mother's Crusade Keeps Man in Prison

Six years ago, Dorothy Story moved out of her parents' home to begin her life as a single adult. Within three months she had been raped and killed. Dorothy's mother lamented, "They [the rapists] cheated her out *of everything*. She was going to beauty school. . . . And when we used to talk, she told me that she wanted to have a family someday and live in a red brick house."[12]

That article demonstrated how strongly Havinghurst's agenda has been accepted by our culture. Terry Campbell, Leavenworth County Sheriff, wrote to the parole board, "A young girl has been denied the joys of life, *having a family* and many wonderful experiences that life has to offer."

Death is a reality that has to be faced. Measuring up is a process or journey, not a destination. At times a crucible with searing heat; at times the chill of loneliness. But at all times, in *all* situations, the faithful presence and guidance of One who has loved us from that first moment He thought of us.

Mordecai prodded Esther as she faced a crucial decision—one that could threaten her life or prevent the annihilation of her people. "Who knows but that *you* have come to royal position for such a time *as this?*" (Esther 4:14) Remove the *you* and insert your name in that verse. That's what I wanted to reply to the writer of this letter:

> I'm thirty years old and have been standing on the edge of life, looking in. I've never been married. I've never had a boyfriend, never had a Friday night date, never gone steady, never been to a drive-in; never had a man to say that he loved me.
>
> That's a long list of *never's!* I came to this conference to find ways to cure some of this deep-seated hurt. Somehow, all the things that were supposed to happen as a teenager never happened to me. All the things I'm supposed to know about . . . I never learned. Or probably never allowed myself to learn. There's that word again—*never.*
>
> Have you ever been down this road? How can I get on with living before life passes me by?

To this single adult—one of God's possibilities—I offer *Positively Single*. Paul encouraged the Ephesians, "Be very careful, then, how you live—not as unwise but as wise, *making the most of every opportunity*" (Eph. 5:15-16).

The secret of successful single living is not self-sufficiency, but sufficiency in Christ Jesus. Singleness is an opportunity to become all that God dreams for us to be.

But the opportunity must be seized. This opportunity will furnish you with the raw resources for the ultimate question that Joseph Aldrich asked in *Love for All Your Worth,* "When you come to the end of your life and have nothing but death to look forward to and nothing but memories to look back upon, what will you need to see to conclude that your life was a success and you are satisfied?"[13]

Are you too "standing on the edge of life," waiting? Or are you fulfilling God's purpose for your life?

QUESTIONS

1. Take a moment to study Havinghurst's list of the developmental tasks of adulthood. Rearrange them in *your* order:

1. ______________________________

2. ______________________________

3. ______________________________

4. ______________________________

5. ______________________________

6. ______________________________

7. ______________________________

8. ______________________________

In what order do you hope to list these items in two years? In five years?

2. The National Committee on Mental Hygiene has composed a list of characteristics of a healthy adult. Circle the appropriate responses that describe you.

yes	no	uncertain	accepts responsibility for his own growth and for contributing to the welfare of others.
yes	no	uncertain	feels that he is a genuine member of the group in which he functions.
yes	no	uncertain	is inquisitive and aggressive without being pugnacious and offensive.
yes	no	uncertain	is an active participant in life.
yes	no	uncertain	gains increasing control over the expression of one's negative feelings: especially anger or fear.
yes	no	uncertain	is secure in importance and acceptance and does not make undue demands for the attention of others.
yes	no	uncertain	has come to terms with one's own body and any physical limitations.
yes	no	uncertain	seeks to grow and improve; to seek self-actualization; is not content with the mere satisfaction of basic needs
yes	no	uncertain	reacts with resistance to temporary stress, contradictions, and disappointments.
yes	no	uncertain	relates positively to others; wins friends, engenders approval, is accepted as a worthy person.

yes no uncertain becomes increasingly independent in thoughts and actions . . . is willing to stand one's own ground.

yes no uncertain is able to accept [himself] and is content to be what [he] is and what [he] is becoming.

yes no uncertain while independent in thought and action, is bounded by consideration of the expectations and mores of society.

yes no uncertain recognizes his own competencies and is willing to accept direction when facing situations in which one is competent.[14]

Look over your answers carefully. Are you comfortable with your answers? Maybe you're skeptical. Or did you moan, "If this is what it means to be an adult, I'll never make it!"

3. Review the three questions from Alan Jones. Can you honestly answer yes to each of these questions? If not, why not? As you continue reading this book, periodically review these three questions.

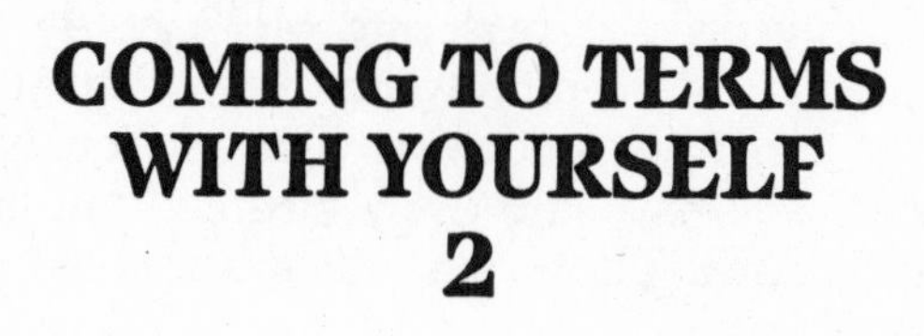

COMING TO TERMS WITH YOURSELF

2

Lately, I have felt a growing concern for what some term *self-talk* or what we say to ourselves. Tragically, I say some things to me and use a tone of voice with myself that I would never use with you. Often I edit my verbal self-putdowns because someone might hear me and challenge my conclusions.

But in my brain there is no filter. My self-talk is undiluted, full-strength, poisonous:

I'm no good!
I can't. . . .
Who would ever love me?
I'm a failure!
I'm too fat!

A person has to be careful. If you go around talking out loud to yourself, the men in white coats will lock you up. But what about those statements that we repeat in the corridors of our hearts—statements that no one else hears? Those words and phrases can cripple. Like acid, they attack the delicate linings of our self-esteem.

Before his conversion Paul was "breathing out murderous threats against the Lord's disciples" (Acts 9:1). Picture him on the road to Damascus—rehearsing his words, practicing his timing. No doubt Paul applauded his own piety. After all, he thought he was doing a noble thing: defending THE faith. Then, as he neared Damascus, he encountered the light: "Saul, Saul, why do you persecute Me?" (v. 4)

Interestingly, the men "traveling with Paul stood there speechless" (v. 7). How paradoxical! Though Paul had lost his sight, he could still have effectively breathed out his threats. But he couldn't see. Those who *could* see couldn't explain what they saw.

I would like to focus on three priorities Paul suggested as reasonable aspects of coming to terms with ourselves. Every single should:

"*Learn to control* his own body in a way that is holy and honorable, not in passionate lust like the heathen" (1 Thes. 4:4-5).

"*Learn to devote* themselves to doing what is good" (Titus 3:14).

Learn "to be content whatever the circumstances" (Phil. 4:11).

LEARN TO CONTROL OUR BODIES

Single adults must learn to control their bodies in order to avoid wronging their brothers or sisters by taking advantage of them (1 Thes. 4:6). Paul, as a single adult, learned to discipline his body. Why? Paul discovered that his body was "the temple of the Holy Spirit." He scolded the Corinthians, "Do you not know that your body is a temple of the Holy Spirit, who is in you, whom you have received from God?" (1 Cor. 6:19)

Paul went a step further, explaining that we are not our own. Contrary to the popular opinion and the anthem of so many single adults, "I did it *my* way" or "I've got to be me," Paul reminded the Corinthians, "You were bought at a price. Therefore honor God with your body" (v. 20).

Traditionally, we have limited this verse to a sexual dimension: "Don't fornicate or commit adultery!" But what about the other, equally offensive and destructive ways of dishonoring our bodies? What about stress? Overeating? Lack of sleep? Lack of exercise? Dr. R.T. Williams observed that for every insult you heap on your body, it will seek and find its ultimate revenge![1] Many single adults overindulge their bodies. Their behavior reflects a low assessment of the value of the temple and therefore the Holy Spirit who inhabits that temple.

Paul declared, "It is God's will that *you* should be holy (1 Thes. 4:3). He could have said "that *we* be holy," but he deliberately used *you*. Our second concern is with the word *holy*. If the passage read, "God's will that you be *good*," we could live with that. But *holy*? Where I live? Where I work? As a single adult with active hormones? Yes.

"Oh," you protest, "I can't be holy." Then you list a dozen reasons why. Yet Paul's statement resonates: "It is God's will that *you* be holy." No footnotes or asterisks that say "with the following exceptions." Paul's *you* includes you!

"But Paul, be reasonable. This is Singleland. Eighties style. Surely it's worse than in New Testament days."

Surely, Paul as a single adult, experienced sexual longing. I don't think his hormones were evaporated by the Damascus Road experience. Yet this single man insisted on no compromise on moral standards.

Why was Paul so insistent? He no doubt agreed with Peter. "[God's] divine power has given us everything we need for life and godliness through our knowledge of Him who called us by His own glory and goodness" (2 Peter 1:3).

Are you saying things to yourself that encourage holy living and self-control?

LEARN TO DO GOOD

Many single adults believe the chief priority on their agendas should be finding their Prince or Princess Charming. He or she is the passport to the land of fulfilling married life and Christian service.

But singleness is more than a hunting season. It is a time to grow, to stretch, to conquer, and to learn. Some of us are not ready for marriage because we have not learned the essentials. We have not mastered those resources which are vital to the survival and growth of a marriage.

Michele Pillar said in *Christian Life:*

> The Christian walk is a constant challenge to allow the Lord to keep us balanced—to walk when it's time to walk and to wait when it's time to wait. . . . God began showing me these things as an example of how we need to give Him time and not rush things on our own.[2]

While we are saved by grace, there ought to be good works in our lives. As single adults our faith must bear fruit. Paul understood this because he traveled from place to place before 800-number reservation systems. In his writings we find "thank-you" notes to individuals for their hospitality. Paul insisted, "Share with God's people who are in need. Practice hospitality" (Rom. 12:13).

Contemporary single adults often overlook the example of the early church. "*All* the believers were together and had everything in common. Selling their possessions and goods, they gave *to anyone* as he had need" (Acts 2:44-45).

Moreover, there were "*no* needy persons among them. For from time to time those who owned lands or houses sold them, brought the money from the sales and put it at the apostles' feet, and it was distributed *to anyone* as he had need" (4:34-35). No wonder the early church turned the world upside down! Not with armies or rhetoric, but with commitment and compassion.

Single adults can lead productive lives contradicting the stereotypes of the "swinging single." Singles generally have more time to invest in careers or recreation. Business rewards such commitment with raises, bonuses, and promotions. But we must also constantly alert ourselves to the danger of "unproductive spiritual lives." God calls *all* of His children—married or single—to ministry and endows all of His children with ministry gifts.

Perhaps you've decided, "I'm waiting until I'm married to get involved in ministry." But what about Paul's nudge, "learn to devote yourself to doing what is good"? No marital qualifications there.

Are you saying to yourself things that encourage you to do good?

LEARN TO BE CONTENT

Paul stated, "I have learned to be content whatever the circumstances" (Phil. 4:11). Look at the circumstances Paul endured:

> I have worked much harder, been in prison more frequently, been flogged more severely, been exposed to death again and again. Five times I received from the Jews the forty lashes minus one. Three times I was beaten with rods, once I was stoned, three times I was shipwrecked, I spent a night and a day in the open sea, I have been constantly on the move. I have been in danger from rivers, in danger from bandits, in danger from my own countrymen, in danger from Gentiles; in danger in the city, in danger in the country, in danger at sea; and in danger from false brothers. I have labored and toiled and have often gone without sleep; I have known hunger and thirst and have often gone without food; I have been cold and naked (2 Cor. 11:23-27).

Despite all that, Paul remained confident in any and all circumstances. Any of us might have survived one or two of these terrors. But Paul survived them all—because he had learned to be content.

Some single adults pride themselves about being able to "take" whatever life dishes out. There are those few who apparently don't need anyone. They would have made great Stoics. Robert Wicks commented that in this passage Paul was not complaining about his life. Paul used the word *autarkes,* a favorite phrase among the Stoics who believed that man possessed the intrinsic ability to resist all external pressures.[3]

Initially, a Stoic might nod in agreement. The Stoics held themselves to be self-sufficient. Paul, however, explained his sufficiency not to be in himself but in Another who strengthened him. That One, who having been single, understands you and equips you for your season of servanthood.

Paul's statement *I have learned* means, in essence, "I have been initiated." Within pagan religions were sub-cults in which only a few members participated. While the public ceremonies were open to all, these "mysteries" were reserved for a few who had learned the secrets or been initiated.

In our search for contentment, some singles race from one seminar to the next, being "initiated" into one super-achiever's philosophy after another. We memorize, we underline, we visualize, but happiness and meaning delude our grasp. Eventually we discover the latest system won't meet our needs. We sink in disappointed depression or resentment.

We need to remember that the secret of successful single adult living is not self-sufficiency but sufficiency in Jesus (Phil. 4:13). Let me offer six secrets of successful single living.

1. *I will learn to reject the materialistic view of success.* When we want to learn a new game such as racquetball, we first have to learn the rules. Rules are as important as techniques. How many single adults measure themselves continuously against a secular yardstick of success? How many of us label ourselves *failures* or *losers* because we have "ring around the collar" instead of "ring around the finger"? How many of us "flirt" with the "swinging single" image and lifestyle?

How many single adults are attempting to define themselves by what they have accumulated? Or by impressive titles? Or by their address? Is success

- what I own?
- what I wear?
- what I drive?
- where I live?
- what I do?

If so, someone always has the bigger/better/newest/latest/most improved—and that fuels covetousness on a grand scale.

Daniel, a single adult, "*resolved* not to defile himself with the royal food and wine" (Dan. 1:8). Daniel made a decision not to eat and enjoy the king's catering, first, because it was not kosher. But he also made that decision because it was a symbol that he had "arrived" socially and politically.

Daniel had learned that lesson early on his spiritual journey. When he interpreted the King's dream and avoided death, the King became an ancient Monte Hall and distributed his loot to Daniel. But Daniel wasn't swayed. Look at his response: "You may keep your gifts for yourself and give your rewards to someone else" (5:17). How many of us would have been that bold?

Some of the loneliest, some of the weirdest, some of the most frustrated single adults are those who drive the newest cars, wear the most fashionable clothes, have the latest hairstyles, straightest teeth, etc. They are trapped on an economic treadmill by a commitment to this world's standards of success. If you are going to grow as a single adult, you must say to yourself, *I am learning to reject the materialistic view of success.*

2. *I will learn to define my life by means other than my job.* What do you hear yourself saying about your work or vocation? "Oh, I'm just a __________." One of the first questions singles ask is, "What do you do?" We assign a pecking order for the response. If the person responds, "I drive a garbage truck," we answer, "Oh, how nice. . . ." without a hint of enthusiasm. However, if he says he is an orthopedic surgeon, we add exclamation marks: "Oh! *How* nice!"

When Daniel's enemies persuaded the king to ban public prayer, the move was aimed to snarl Daniel. Daniel didn't learn about the king's order on the "CBS Evening News." Nor did it particularly rattle him. Daniel didn't become unglued or wring his hands; he *knew* how he would respond. "He went home to his upstairs room where the windows opened toward Jerusalem. Three times a day he got down on his knees and prayed, giving thanks to his God, *just as he had done before*" (Dan. 6:10). Habit led to obedience, even in crisis.

Do you have such a stable faith? Remember in Daniel's case we're not just talking about unemployment, but a forced retirement with no severance pay, no luncheon, no gold watch. Daniel didn't *have* to open those windows to pray. He could have prayed while doing leg lifts or sit-ups—incognito. He could have camouflaged his faith. Though Daniel realized he stood to lose his prophetic franchise, he defined his life by obedience—*not* by his occupation. That's spiritual stability!

No spiritual hand-wringing, no anxiety attacks. Merely the cool, calm action of one man who had learned to be content whatever the circumstances.

If you are going to grow as a Christian single, you will constantly have to repeat, *I am learning to define myself in ways other than by my vocation.*

3. *I will learn to treat all people with dignity.* Single adult groups attract misfits like honey draws flies. But single adults are often quick to judge and discard. Singles can give that once-over glance and then dare anyone to cross into their territorial waters. Most nerds have never learned to translate body English, so they get blasted with the heavy artillery of rejection.

By this point in our lives, many of us have been scarred by past rejections. We have been the brunt of too many jokes and snide comments. We can't cope with any more rejections. Being rejected by a singles' group may be the last straw.

James gives a stern warning against showing favoritism based on a person's appearance:

> Suppose a [single] comes into your meeting wearing a gold ring and fine clothes, and a poor man in shabby clothes also comes in. If you show special attention to the [single] wearing fine clothes and say, "Here's a good seat for you," but say to the poor [single], "You stand there" or "Sit on the floor by my feet," have you not discriminated among yourselves and become judges with evil thoughts? (James 2:3-4)

Everyone deserves to be treated with dignity. If you are going to grow as a Christian and as a single adult, you will have to hear yourself saying, *I am learning to treat all people as persons with dignity, worth, and value.*

4. *I will learn to be a good steward of my talents.* Some single adults covet ministry gifts. We have so overpraised the ministry gifts of certain celebrities that we have ignored the equally bestowed gifts of others, equally talented, but lesser known. If it's a choice between buying Belinda Swartz's new cassette and Celebrity X's, whose will it be? If you have to

choose between Elmer Fotz's new book and Celebrity Y's, whose book will you buy?

God *does* give some people dynamic, dramatic, highly visible ministries. That does not mean that He loves them any more than He loves the rest of us. Look again at Daniel. When the King was ready to nix his entire regiment of wise men, Arioch interrupted, "I have found a man among the exiles from Judah" (which is inaccurate since Daniel had found Arioch) "who can tell the king what his dream means" (Dan. 2:25).

Suddenly, Daniel was thrust center stage. Though he had ministered in his apprenticeship in a prison cell, he was now ready to play the palace at "prime time." His opportunity had come at last.

First, Daniel set the record straight. "As for me, this mystery has been revealed to me," [and I doubt that he punctuated the statement with a slap to the chest] "not because I have greater wisdom than other living men, but so that you, O King, may know the interpretation and that you may understand what went through your mind" (v. 30).

Learn to be a good steward of your talents, in whatever arena you find yourself. If you are going to grow as a Christian, you will have to say to yourself repeatedly (and sometimes before, during, and after a service or concert), *I am learning to be a good steward of my talents.*

5. *I will learn to extract good from every situation.* Have you heard the story of the boy whose sadistic parents gave him a ton of manure for Christmas? Though his brothers were excited about their toys, this kid was not complaining. He was jumping up and down! Why the optimism? "With all this manure," the tyke squealed, "there's got to be a pony somewhere!"

All of us get portions of the good, the bad, and the ugly. Unfortunately, some people get more than a fair share of the latter two. But a creative single adult *learns* to take the bad and turn it into good with the help of Christ. Who can forget Joseph's words to his cold-hearted brothers, "You meant evil against me, but God meant it for good" (Gen. 50:20, NASB).

Because Daniel explained the king's dreams, the king appointed him to a high position and "lavished many gifts on him." Moreover, he "placed him in charge" of all the wise men (Dan. 2:48). But though "the getting was good," Daniel remembered his friends. He requested that the king honor Shadrach, Meshach, and Abednego too (v. 49).

Paul observed, "*In all things* God works for the good of those who love Him, who have been called according to His purpose" (Rom. 8:28). There is nothing that can happen to you but that God will help you work through it.

To be a mature Christian, you need to develop long-term vision. You will constantly have to remind yourself, *I am learning to extract good in every situation.*

6. *I will learn to develop a network of cheerleaders.* As I was growing up, I was a Saturday morning devotee of the TV parade of great single adults: the Lone Ranger, Pete and Jim on "Fury," and Sky King. Yet even the Lone Ranger had "his faithful sidekick, Tonto." How many times did Tonto bring Kimosabe through the threat of death? These were no macho heroes riding into the sunset singing, "I did it my way!"

Daniel, in his crisis over the king's dream, promptly "explained the matter *to his friends*" and "urged them to plead for mercy from the God of heaven" (Dan. 2:17-18). Thus, in his crisis Daniel relied on an existing network of friends.

Single adults need people who love them, despite what their friends know about them. A Jewish proverb says it well: "One enemy is too many; but a hundred friends are not enough." The author of Ecclesiastes observed:

> There was a man all alone; he had neither son nor brother. There was no end to his toil, yet his eyes were not content with his wealth. "For whom am I toiling," he asked, "and why am I depriving myself of enjoyment?" This too is meaningless—a miserable business!
>
> Two are better than one, because they have a good return for their work; if one falls down, his friend can help him up. But pity the man who falls, and has no one to help him up! (Ecc. 4:8-10)

If you are going to grow as a Christian single, ***you will have to develop a network of faithful friends.***

CONCLUSION

Learning is an unending task. Remember your mother or father demanding, "When will you *ever* learn?" or "When will you get this through your thick head?"

What do you hear yourself saying to yourself? How are you coming to terms with yourself?

In today's success-saturated society, God is still looking for single adults, like Daniel, whether male or female, young or old, who are willing to learn His lessons. Willing to serve the vigorous apprenticeship. In every generation, God's giants have come to terms with themselves by learning to:

control their bodies,
devote themselves to doing good,
be content in their circumstances.

COMING TO TERMS WITH YOUR BODY
3

"I think I have an inferiority complex," a man complained to a psychologist.

"Sit down and tell me about it," the counselor said. After a series of "Hmm's" and "I see's," the client was told to return two weeks later.

When he did, he again talked about his sense of inferiority. For months, the pattern continued.

Finally, the psychologist said, "I have good news for you."

The client grinned in expectation.

"You *don't* have an inferiority complex," the counselor announced.

"I don't?" the man gasped.

"No. You really *are* inferior!"

This story strikes home with thousands of single adults who live in a world that hawks breath mints, deodorants, mouthwashes, toothpastes, and soaps as essential for social survival.

Health clubs are doing a booming business reshaping old bodies. Some promise results without an ounce of sweat. For those with persistent areas your health club can't fix, a plastic surgeon will help.

Many single adults while watching television, especially

the commercials, moan, "I wish my ________ were __________." Or, "If only my breasts were (smaller/larger/fuller) *then*. . . ." Or, "If only my hair were (longer/shorter/silkier) *then*. . . ." Few of us can accept ourselves "warts and all."

Inferiority complexes run in a vicious cycle and may have disastrous consequences. David Seamands notes that inferiority complexes paralyze potential, destroy dreams, ruin relationships, and sabotage service to the kingdom.[1] Sometimes, they are passed to the next generation as an emotional heirloom.

You have probably discovered that to get rid of your inferiority complex you can't just clap your hands and yell, "Scat!" An inferiority complex is a pushy tenant. You will have to evict it—and it will fight you all the way.

ORIGINS OF THE INFERIORITY

Inferiority complexes begin early in life. It's natural to compare our bodies, our skills, and our abilities with those of siblings or playmates. Adolescent growth spurts compound the problem. Eventually we must become comfortable with our bodies and get on with life's agenda. Yet, some singles get stuck comparing and coveting. They become specialists in comparison. "If only" is their constant lament.

Victims of inferiority complexes oversensitize themselves to one particular offensive body part. "If only I could change that one part." Almost everyone they meet prompts an immediate comparison. Dr. Irwin Ross insists that it takes intelligence to have an inferiority complex. "To perceive the merits of others and compare them with your own" is hard work. "You compare yourself *as a whole* with just one or two special virtues in another."[2]

In the Old Testament, the Jews placed great emphasis on physical strength. People with any sort of handicap faced social discrimination and stigma. The Jews didn't set aside special parking spaces for handicapped chariot drivers. In fact, some wondered, "Who sinned? The handicapped person or his parents?"

Once David had solidified his kingdom, he remembered his commitment to Jonathan. He asked, "Is there no one still left of the house of Saul to whom I can show God's kindness?" (2 Sam. 9:3)

Ziba, a servant, answered, "There is still a son of Jonathan; he is crippled in both feet" (v. 3). Because of the Jewish emphasis on physical strength, though Mephibosheth had royal blood, his handicap kept him from being perceived as a threat to David. Some could have argued that the kingship should have passed through the bloodline. But who would follow a lame prince?

Mephibosheth had been in exile in Lo Debar until David summoned him to the palace. The summons must have frightened the prince because he realized that he could be killed as a threat to David. In many countries newly appointed leaders often execute or exile the offspring of the previous leaders.

When David met the boy he exclaimed, "Mephibosheth!" David urged him not to be afraid. "I will restore to you *all* the land that belonged to your grandfather Saul, and you will always eat at my table" (v. 7). That's not a bad deal. In essence, David was promising, "Even if there is a crop failure, you will have a place at my table."

Mephibosheth should have been ecstatic. But look at his response: "What is your servant, that you should notice a dead dog like me?" (v. 8) How is that for a positive self-image?

You've seen a dead dog lying in the middle of the highway. A repulsive sight. Generally, you try not to look at it. Yet, here the grandson of the former king of Israel called himself "a dead dog." How many sons and daughters of the King of kings use similar synonyms to put down themselves?

Let's examine five traits of single adults with inferiority complexes.

1. *Single adults with inferiority complexes rely on others to be their mirrors.* Remember how you longed for puberty? There was something so spectacular about that period of our lives. Trying to anticipate pimples; desperately seeking the approval of others. Wanting to look cool—whatever that

meant. Enduring fads and styles, to say nothing of parental disapproval.

Thoreau said, "Some of us must march to the tune of a different drummer." Many biological adults have never become emotional/spiritual adults because they rely on peer pressure for direction. The "crowd" makes their decisions. They look to advertisers for what they should wear. *Whatever you say* is their motto.

Some people whose bodies are not genetically predisposed to Calvin Klein fashions stuff themselves into his designs. Why? They saw Brooke Shields or Tom Selleck or some other celebrity wearing Product X and transferred that person's sensuality to that product. So they reason, *If I wear Calvin Klein jeans, everyone will notice me.*

2. *Singles with inferiority complexes are perfectionists and have unrealistic expectations.* Did you take piano lessons? Can you play now? If you're like me, you took from Miss Helen's Perfectionistic School of Piano Technique. Remember those wonderful (?) hours spent practicing scales? Or little ditties for one or two fingers?

Suppose your day at grade school had been great. On the bus ride home you made plans to do something stimulating like watching "Leave It to Beaver." Bam! The thought hit you: *Oh, no! I've got to practice the piano!* Sometimes, to make it worse, a friend would invite you over.

"Can't do it," you'd mumble.

"Why not?" the friend persisted.

"I have to . . . uh," you stalled (it was worse for guys). "I have to do something."

Sometimes you probably argued with your mother. "Mother of mine, I do not wish to practice today."

Most mothers used one of three responses:

THE BOLD:	"Get in there. Now! I don't want to hear another word."
THE HURT:	"Well, (sniff) I suppose it's OK . . . if you (sniff) don't want to practice. Someday you'll wish you had."

THE MARTYR: "Look at all I'm giving up so that you can take piano lessons."

Perhaps you made it all the way to the big recital. You knew your piece perfectly. But somehow in the excitement, you messed up. So you started over again. Why? You thought you had to play it perfectly. But by trying to play those pieces perfectly, some of us grew to hate the piano.

Too early most of us learned that even mild criticism wounds. We learned that if we did something perfectly, we significantly reduced the potential for criticism. Anything less than perfect, however, made us "sitting ducks."

3. *Singles with inferiority complexes have more than their fair percentage of scar tissue.* When I was a teen, my pastor bragged that the youth were "the church of tomorrow." He tested that idea by organizing teen musical ensembles.

I still remember the night the boys quartet sang. Our hearts beat rapidly as the pastor introduced us. We had practiced—we *really* had. We had our song down pat.

But somehow, the pianist started in one key and we were in four other keys with four different tempos. Then Ron's voice cracked as teenage boys' voices are prone to do. We should have stopped and started over. But we went on.

By the second verse the potential for blessing by our musical efforts had been greatly reduced. On the third verse we looked to the youth group, hoping that our peers were lifting us up in prayer. Instead, they were snickering and laughing—forgetting that next week it would be their turn.

On the fourth verse we glanced at our parents who were staring at the floor. After we finished, there was a long silent moment. Finally the pastor mumbled, "Didn't you appreciate the uh . . . *words* of that song?"

That hurt. The boys in the quartet agreed that we could live without that kind of humiliation, so we vowed "never again!"

Why don't single adults assume more responsibility? Sometimes it's because they've tried in the past and failed, and they can't forget it. They reason, *I might fail again, so I'd better not try.*

4. *Singles with inferiority complexes covet.* "If only I had her ________, then I'd be dating!" How do you fill in the blank?

The tenth commandment declares, "You shall not covet." Moses got specific: "Your neighbor's house or wife, his manservant or maidservant, his ox or donkey."

Some single adults have ugly neighbors, so that's no real temptation. Few of us have neighbors who have servants. So we don't have to worry about that. And not many of us would want an ox or donkey living with us. So we're in the clear, right? We have nothing to covet.

But what about Moses' catch-all phrase: "*Or anything that belongs to your neighbor*"? (Ex. 20:17, NASB) It's possible to covet your neighbor's tan, or his IRA, or his racquetball skills. Or education or charm. Or dating life.

How easily in a materialistic world we allow ourselves to be impressed by the success of others. Ironically, we are always stunned by the suicide of someone we assumed "had it all."

Saul illustrates this point. He appeared to have it all. Physically, he was "an impressive young man without equal among the Israelites—a head taller than any of the others" (1 Sam. 9:2). But when he was chosen king, he was found hiding "among the baggage" (10:22). Samuel cried, "Do you see the man the Lord has chosen? There is no one like him among the people" (v. 24).

However, if we examine the reaction *after* David had killed Goliath, we find a paradox. All the women "came out . . . to meet King Saul with singing and dancing. . . . As they danced, they sang, 'Saul has slain his thousands' " (18:6-7). Picture Saul enjoying the parade until the women sang verse two: "And David his tens of thousands." What a public relations fiasco!

"Saul was very angry; this refrain galled him. 'They have credited David with tens of thousands,' he thought, 'but me with only thousands. What more can he get but the kingdom?' And from that time on Saul kept a jealous eye on David" (vv. 8-10).

What? Saul the king coveted the success of David? Saul could have challenged Goliath any of those forty mornings or evenings when the giant insulted him (17:16). Besides, giant-killing was hardly enough on a resumé to threaten the current king. But Saul was afraid "because the Lord was with David" (18:12). And "all Israel and Judah loved David, because he led them in their campaigns" (18:16).

Saul tried to sabotage David by inviting him to become his son-in-law. We get a unique insight into David's inferiority: "Who am I, and what is my family or my father's clan in Israel," he exclaimed, "that I should become the king's son-in-law?' " (18:18) Later, Saul hoped his daughter Michal would become a snare to David. He said, "Now you have a second opportunity to become my son-in-law" (v. 21). Saul passed the word through the grapevine: "Speak to David privately and say, 'Look, the king is pleased with you, and his attendants all like you; now become his son-in-law'," (v. 22).

David repeated his previous excuse. "Do you think it is a small matter to become the king's son-in-law? I'm only a poor man and little known" (18:23). *Little known?* There's David's inferiority again. He was on all of the "Top 40" charts (all the women were singing about him) and all "Israel and Judah loved him." Yet, inferiority complexes often are not reasonable or logical.

5. *Single adults with inferiority complexes take themselves too seriously.* What happens when you pass a three-way mirror? Is it a friend or foe?

Some of us are overly self-conscious. "Don't tease me about my ________. That's off limits!" For example, I'm losing my hair and am somewhat uptight about that. Just once I wish a woman could run her fingers through my hair (she would have to have thin fingers!). I see men with scads of hair and I think, *If only.*

I can grow hair on my chest—no problem there. Some one suggested that the hormones obviously aren't getting to the top floor. Of course, there are plenty of ads hawking solutions, but they affect my wallet more than my scalp.

Besides, what's wrong with baldness? Look what it has

done for Telly Savalas. Is he lonely?

A genetic code deep within me has predisposed me to baldness. I have to accept that. But in the meantime, I need to be able to laugh about my receding hairline. That's only one insignificant part of me. It's what's under the scalp that counts!

ALTERNATIVES TO INFERIORITY

By this point, you are probably saying, "I knew all that. Give me some solutions or alternatives."

First, *concentrate on the key item of your inferiority.* Ask yourself three key questions:

- Can I do anything about my inferiority?
- If I can, am I willing to pay the price?
- If I cannot, am I willing to change my attitude toward my inferiority?

My college roommate had muscles on his muscles; I had flab on my flab. I weighed 275 pounds and was assigned to room with a weight lifter. They called him "the incredible hulk" and me "the incredible bulk."

That guy made my life miserable. His "If only you would's" devastated me. Actually, my problem was big bones. Some people are fat. I am big-boned!

Secondly, I blamed my weight on my mother. After tough, mentally excruciating days learning long division, I was ready for a snack. I'd come home, drained. It was all I could do to make it through the backdoor. And mother always had "after school" treats. Of course, she would say, "Now don't eat too many. We don't want to spoil your appetite."

But eventually I had to take the responsibility for my problem. My weight was not my mother's fault. I had chosen to weigh what I weighed. I had to assume personal responsibility. No more excuses. I would have to eat like a person who weighed 185 pounds.

You have to take the responsibility to find a solution to your feelings of inferiority. Can you change? By exercise? By diet? By surgery?

Grin and bear it. Shortcomings can be a springboard to success. Look at country music singer Mel Tillis who stutters. He doesn't stutter when he sings. Or Terry Foxx, the Canadian runner who developed cancer. When he had his leg amputated, he ran on an artificial leg. When his second leg had to be amputated, he ran on the stubs.

Sometimes, to grin and bear it you'll need to take a long look (however painful) in the mirror and befriend the offensive item. Make friends with your inferiority stimulator. Blaine Smith explained this process in *One of a Kind:*

> In every area where I felt myself to be gifted, I quickly realized that there were other students who surpassed me. There seemed to be nothing I could hang my hat on identity wise, nothing that made me distinctive. For a while that was depressing, and I found myself going through the worst identity crisis I had ever experienced.
>
> The day came, however, when a simple thought that has been life changing suddenly occurred to me. It dawned on me that no matter how hard I worked, I would always find someone who was a better guitarist; no matter how hard I worked, I would always find someone who was a better teacher; no matter how hard I worked, I would always find someone who was a better student. No matter what the talent was and no matter how hard I worked at developing it, I was always going to find others who could surpass me at that point.[3]

Maybe you can identify with that. But look at his marvelous discovery: "But no matter how far and wide I looked, I would never find another person who had my same gifts *in the same combination*. In this sense I am utterly unique."[4]

That makes so much sense. Some of the most beautiful Hollywood celebrities need easy lines to memorize. Their brains are not the most developed parts of their bodies.

Substitution. There are some things that I cannot do and will never be able to do. I could read possibility thinking books until I croaked, but there are still things I cannot achieve. I have to *honestly* assess my abilities, strengths, and desires.

For example, I could never make a living on my musical talents. Though I like to sing and play the piano and organ, I have to honestly admit that I will never give Dino or Van Cliburn a run for their money. But then Dino is not a speaker or writer. *Admit your limitations or handicaps.*

"Others are seldom giving the attention to the particular aspect of our appearance that we are dwelling on. They see us not as one characteristic but as a *combination,* not as a part but as a whole."[5]

Everyone has limitations. *Everyone,* even those people we see as the most skilled, talented, or glamorous. The wise simply learn more quickly how to deal with their inadequacies.

I once attended an organ concert at Scarritt College. The skilled artist had played for an hour. He had one last piece to play before he took his ovation and his honorarium. However, I noticed on the last selection that he fidgeted with the organ stops. He started, then stopped. Finally, he played. Later, I learned that the organ had misfunctioned and an F# would not sound.

If that had been a lot of us, we would have thrown the music in the air, pulled our hair, and flailed the console with our cummerbunds. But this professional transposed the music and played the selection in a different key.

That's what you have to do occasionally with life. Transpose. Learn to discipline your emotional reactions to your limitations and inferiorities.

Thank God for what you do have. It is so easy to schedule a mini-pity party. "Poor me! If only . . . " Be patient—God is still at work.

Many times my attention has been drawn to a verse in Isaiah: "The images that are carried about are burdensome, a burden for the weary" (Isa. 46:1). I understand that. My inferiority feelings sometimes get heavy. Generally, I am afraid to mention them. If I told you what I feel inferior about, you'd probably laugh.

But deep inside me, I'm having a terrible struggle evicting my inferiority complex. While I no longer weigh 275 pounds, some of those old thoughts still taunt me: *Look at you! You're a mess! Who would want to go out with you?*

But I am changing. I've at least gotten the complex out of its room, down the hall, and closer to the exit.

God didn't make me perfect. I'm not going to wake up with a head of hair that would qualify me for shampoo commercials. But the money I save on barbers (and toupees) I can spend on ice cream cones.

God doesn't call only the perfect—the beautiful—the talented. Look over this "Who's Who" of inferiority:

King Saul	I was afraid of the people and so I gave in to them (1 Sam. 15:24).
Jacob	I am unworthy of all the kindness and faithfulness You have shown Your servant (Gen. 32:10).
Abraham	I am nothing but dust and ashes (Gen. 18:27).
Isaiah	I am a man of unclean lips, and I live among a people of unclean lips (Isa. 6:5).
Gideon	How can I save Israel? My clan is the weakest in Manasseh, and I am the least in my family (Jud. 6:15).
Moses	O Lord, I have never been eloquent, neither in the past nor since You have spoken to Your servant. I am slow of speech and tongue (Ex. 4:10).
Amos	I was neither a prophet nor a prophet's son, but I was a shepherd,

> and I also took care of sycamore fig trees (Amos 7:14).

Yet these individuals each found a niche in God's design.

VICTORY OVER INFERIORITY

You can have victory over your inferiority. Perhaps not overnight. It's like a bank investment. It takes as much effort and energy to dismantle it as it took to construct it. Besides, you've probably nourished it.

I must ask myself:

- Am I going to allow this to sabotage my service?
- Am I going to allow this to paralyze my potential?
- Am I going to allow this to destroy my dreams?
- Am I going to allow this to ruin my relationships?

NO! I am healthy. I have talents. I have skills. I have friends. I have creativity. Why should I—with all that—sit around bemoaning the fact that my ________ is not ________?

I think of David Brainerd, missionary to the American Indians, who was troubled by low self-esteem. He wrote, "I verily thought that I was the meanest, vilest, most helpless, guilty, ignorant, benighted creature living."[6]

He too called himself a dead dog. "My soul was grieved for the congregation that they should sit there and hear such a dead dog as I preach." He added, "Yet, I knew what God had done for my soul."[7]

God used David Brainerd, a flawed vessel, to awaken thousands spiritually. He will use you too.

When I was a child, my mother used to say, "Go wash your hands and face." Often, I'd run my hands under the water, then wipe them on the towel. My mother would urge, "Go *wash* your face and hands!" I'd try it again.

The third time she would escort me to the sink. She would soap up the washcloth and wash my face and hands, and sometimes it hurt.

How about you? Are you being gentle with yourself? You know your inferiorities, your flaws. The sources of your discomforts. Do yourself a favor. Evict the tenant. Serve notice today. Ask yourself:

- Can I do anything about my inferiority?
- If I can, am I willing to pay the price?
- If I cannot, am I willing to change my attitude?

Inferiority is a complex subject that's made many mental health care professionals rich. Who knows the single adults who have never achieved their dreams? Their downfall was not cocaine or alcohol or adultery or lack of education or poverty. But an inferiority complex.

Inferiority complexes are heavy. But there is a better way to live. One of the agendas of adulthood is coming to terms with your body and the inferior feelings you may have about yourself.

COMING TO TERMS WITH YOUR PARENTS
4

Howard Halpern in *Cutting Loose: An Adult Guide to Coming to Terms with Your Parents* composed a glossary of "saintly" words and terms commonly used in conversations with parents. Do these sound familiar?

"I am only thinking of what is *best.* . . ."
"*God* told me that you. . . ."
"You should be *grateful.* . . ."
"You should feel *guilty* about. . . ."
"You *must.* . . ."
"We *never.* . . ." or "Well, I *never!*"
"What will *people* say?" or "*People* will talk!"
"I'm not telling you what to do, but *if I were* you. . . ."
"You *shouldn't* feel that way. . . ."
"It's a *shame* the way he. . . ."
"*After all* I've done for you. . . ."

Can you add to the list? Halpern says that parents use such words and phrases to provoke immediate fear and guilt. He continues, "Some of us have been 'blessed' by parents who are saints and we may still be trying to recuperate from the blessing."[1]

One of the first agenda items for single adults is settling this question: What will the nature of my relationship be with my parents: son/daughter or *child*? This issue has to be decided in light of the fifth commandment: "Honor your father and mother, so that you may live long in the land" (Ex. 20:12).

This is becoming more of a problem as parents live longer. Perhaps you can appreciate one father's threat to his children: "I intend to live long enough to give each of you as much misery and joy as you have given me!"

The problem is also complicated by the American tradition that it is the duty of the unmarried daughter or son to take more, if not total, responsibility for aging parents since other siblings have "family" responsibilities.

A close reading of Scripture discloses that this problem is not new. Rarely, however, do we dissect the accounts to study the tense relationships that existed between parents and offspring, particularly fathers and sons. Was there favoritism at work between Adam and Abel that annoyed Cain? Seemingly, there was little or no contact between Adam and Cain after Cain murdered Abel.

Consider the obvious favoritism of Isaac and Rebekah for their twins. "Isaac, who had a taste for wild game, loved Esau, but Rebekah loved Jacob" (Gen. 25:28). That reality led to Jacob's deception. Or consider Joseph's conniving brothers. They had problems with their father. "Israel loved Joseph more than any of his other sons, because he had been born to him in his old age" (37:3). The famous "coat of many colors" only increased the antagonism.

In the New Testament the striking example is Jesus' relationship with Mary and His use of the Parable of the Lost Son. Let's look at some of these accounts in order to discover some helpful principles for dealing with our parents.

GUIDELINE ONE: DECIDE TO BE A SON OR DAUGHTER

Some single adults have formed such strong relationships with one or both of their parents that they cannot become adult sons or daughters. Trapped in childlike dependencies, any challenge or alteration creates stress.

In the last few years the problem of incest has become more public. But few experts talk about emotional/spiritual incest. Too many parents, especially mothers, have formed emotional/spiritual one-flesh relationships with their children. Some parents will give up everything to be chauffeur and friend and companion. They will do without so that their children can have "everything" they didn't have.

What will be the nature of your relationship with your parents? You must decide to be a son or daughter rather than a child. You can be manipulated or shamed or threatened into a continued childship. But it's *your* decision—and God will hold you accountable as an adult.

Some parents want to maintain the child/parent relationship. Some religious teachings encourage a perpetual childship until you marry. The notion persists that you become an adult *when* you marry, not before.

But Scripture says, "A man *will leave* his father and mother and be united to his wife, and they will become one flesh" (Gen. 2:24). Jesus quoted this injunction to the Pharisees (Matt. 19:5); Paul restated it in Ephesians 5. This biblical directive leads to the wording of the wedding vows, "And forsaking *all* others." That includes Mama.

Part of being a successful mature adult is living on your own. During the recent recession, many singles went "running" home to Mom and Dad "to save a few bucks." Some crawled back into the cocoon and haven't left yet.

One of life's major priorities—whether you're married or single—should be severing the emotional umbilical cord with your parents. It is *your* decision. The earlier you make the break, the less complicated the implications. You'll have fewer bad habits to break and fewer bad memories to forget.

GUIDELINE TWO: REJECT YOUR PARENTS' FEARS AND IRRATIONALITIES

At least early in Jesus' ministry, Mary, His mother, attempted to influence Him. At the beginning of His public ministry, Jesus and His mother attended a wedding in Cana where His mother informed Jesus that their host had run out of wine.

Jesus responded, "Dear woman, why do you involve Me?" (John 2:4) However, Mark tells us that at a later point, Jesus' family "went to take charge of Him" having concluded "He is out of His mind" (Mark 3:20-21).

Perhaps Mary feared the audiences—already the hometown folk had tried to kill Him, after He had read Isaiah's words in the synagogue (Luke 4:28-30). Yet, Jesus rejected Mary's fears. When Jesus was told that His mother and brothers were outside, He responded, "Who are My mother and My brothers?" Rather, He retorted, "*Here* are My mother and My brothers!" (Mark 3:33-34) However much He loved Mary, He could not let her fears sabotage His ministry.

By the time we've spent our growing-up years with our family, we tend to either react to, mimic, or reject their biases. One single adult, age 35, called me and asked for help with a major decision. She wanted to go to Europe. "But my mom and Aunt Ethel are pitching one fit!" (For years, the mother had used her health to manipulate her daughter.) The mother had demanded, "What if I die while you're galavanting across Europe?"

You have to let your parents know that you are rejecting their fears and irrationalities—not them. "Go," I suggested. She followed my advice and had a wonderful time.

GUIDELINE THREE: AFFIRM YOUR PARENTS' PROGRESS

Parents can change. "Not mine!" you protest. I remember when my parents believed that the *King James Version* of the Bible was *the* translation. In fact, during college vacations we had some tense conversations on the subject. But twenty years later, my parents read the *New International Version.* I wouldn't have predicted that change.

Parents can change! One November I called home the night of the gubernatorial election. "Your daddy won and I lost," my mom groaned.

Knowing that a woman, Martha Layne Collins, was the Democratic candidate, I was confused. My parents were strong Republicans.

"The woman won!"

"Huh?" Now I was confused. My father is in his seventies and had never voted for a Democrat.

"Can you believe that your father actually voted for a Democrat?" my mother asked.

"And a woman at that," I mumbled. I would never have predicted that change.

We need to affirm and applaud our parents' progress. In some cases that means recognizing even the "baby" steps.

GUIDELINE FOUR: RECOGNIZE YOUR PARENTS' FAULTS AND INADEQUACIES

A lot of single adults describe their parents like this: They're wonderful! I just love to be with them!"

Indeed, that is one reason why some single adults never marry. They are looking for a "daddy" or "mommy" junior.

However, some unmarrieds have placed their parents on a pedestal and have ignored some inconsistencies. Linda Leonard in *The Wounded Woman* observed that often a single woman's relationships to men "are constricted because no man can match their father."[2]

Perhaps you had *the critical judge* father. A father you could never please (though other siblings could). Or you had an *absentee* father who was never there when *you* needed him. As a result, some single adults have poor relationships with their fathers.

Some parents influence even from the grave. In the play, "I Never Sang for My Father," the main character said, "Death ends a life, but it doesn't end a relationship."[3] Linda Leonard commented:

> I really had to look at [my father], to try to understand his side of the story, his aspirations and despair. No longer could I dismiss him from my life as though I could totally escape the past and his influence. Nor could I simply blame him as the cause of my troubles.[4]

Many single adults stagger under a load of fantasy about their parents. You must remember that you were not conceived by two angels or saints, but by two humans. Your denial of their inadequacies may lead to camouflaged faults being passed to a second generation.

How many single adults stagger under a load of fantasy about their parents? Or hope to change them? Consider Joseph's brothers' feelings (they've been bad-mouthed by a lot of preachers and teachers). Their real problem wasn't Joseph or his coat. It was Israel's favoritism. They could only say, "Dad has a favorite." Perhaps, they thought by removing the favored son, their father would be more open toward them. However, Joseph might have been more diplomatic in reporting his dreams and could have cooled off some of their antagonism and jealousy.

The brothers should have acknowledged their father's favoritism. The same is true with Esau's resentment of Rebekah's favoritism of Jacob (Gen. 25:27-28). In both situations, the resentment led to sin.

GUIDELINE FIVE: DETERMINE YOUR POINT OF NO RETURN

Some issues are not worth fighting. They only drain your energy. When I am with my parents, I filter my remarks. Some things get run up the flagpole, but I choose not to salute them. Some parents respect "territorial waters" and ignore certain subjects or personalities. Others rush in where angels fear to tread.

Perhaps you grew up in a strongly opinionated family. Everything merited a personal opinion or "two cents" worth. Sometimes, you must ignore the small issues to concentrate on the major ones.

I suggest that Laban was rather opinionated in his treatment of Jacob. Jacob called his wives, Laban's daughters, out into the field and explained the predicament. The daughters had to admit that Laban had used up their inheritance. They reached a point of no return by saying, "So do whatever God has told you" (Gen 31:16). What a pained confession!

How many times have we felt nudged about some parental attitude and sometimes have defended it. Roommates, dates, and fiancees see through our families so clearly. Sometimes our defense of our families leads to arguments, sharp disagreements, even broken relationships with our friends.

GUIDELINE SIX: RESIST THEIR CURIOSITY

Some parents have an insatiable curiosity about your single life. Those who watch soap operas or read romance novels may even venture to wonder about your sex life. They may have read some recent poll in *Cosmopolitan* or *Mademoiselle* that 89.9 percent of single women are sexually active. Suddenly, Mama is uneasy.

Some parents fudge. "Well, it's nothing to *me* who you are dating. But Mrs. Bernard, my neighbor, was wondering!"

Parents may have a ritual questioning. Every visit or every phone call is an interrogation. Some parents play Columbo. They take a piece of data from one conversation and link it with a piece of data from another. Sometimes they arrive at startling conclusions.

Anticipate your parents' curiosity and decide how much of your day-to-day life you will disclose. Use the old POW routine: name, rank, and serial number.

GUIDELINE SEVEN: REDUCE YOUR MANIPULABILITY

Some parents keep a scoreboard or talley sheet: "After all I've done for you, looks like the *least* you could do is. . . ."

How many times have single adults been manipulated into attending a family reunion, going home for Christmas, spending most of their vacations at home, or rejecting a job offer—because of the ledgerbooks. Some parents *do* go for the jugular. They can selectively remember from the past that which humiliates us. In fact, some parents are so skilled in this style of manipulation that their children will never win.

Esau was manipulated by his resentment toward his brother and his parents. Already Rebekah had announced her dislike of his wives, "I'm disgusted with living because of these Hittite women" (Gen. 27:46). That must have made for some coolish family gatherings. Yet she added, "If Jacob takes a wife from among the women of this land, from Hittite women like these, my life will not be worth living" (v. 46). I think she added an exclamation mark. So after Jacob was blessed and "Esau then realized how despleasing the Canaanite women were to his father," he promptly married another, Mahalath (28:8-9). I doubt if this woman was welcomed with open arms by Rebekah.

One acquaintance cringes every time her father comes for a visit. He looks around her beautiful home and snarls, "Something fishy's going on. You must be cheating on your taxes or tithing to afford this. How could you own this on a schoolteacher's salary?" Instant anger.

Another tactic that keeps many single adults open to manipulation is the trinket. Fringe benefits such as home-cooked meals, Dad picking up your restaurant bills, vacations "as a family," shopping sprees, or down-payments on cars or condos—just to name a few.

The trinkets must be resisted if you are going to be a successful *adult*. Certainly, your parents will want to "do things" for you. But be sure that there is an understanding on hidden expectations and the terms of the gifts.

Most of us can be manipulated at some point. But you must limit your manipulability. Your parents know exactly which buttons to push (but you can disconnect). Sometimes you may have to "grin and bear it" just to break the habit of fighting back.

GUIDELINE EIGHT: DEVELOP YOUR OWN TRADITIONS

Annette Muto in *Celebration of the Single Life* insists that single adults must develop their own traditions, particularly in dealing with the holidays. What do you do for Christmas (by tradition)? Go home to your parents' place? Do you ever wish you could go to the Club Med in Hawaii or to Florida instead? Just once?

Parents protest, "Oh, it wouldn't be Christmas without you!" Maybe they should reread the Christmas story. Some parents threaten, "This *could* be our last Christmas together, you know."

You also need to develop a tradition on parental visits. Your home—whether an apartment, condo, or duplex—is *your* turf. It is not an extension of your parents'. Do your parents have keys to your home? Why? Ah, in case you should fall in the bathtub . . . to prevent the firemen from having to ax down the front door? Do your parents feel free to "drop in"? Anytime? Have your parents ever ambushed a romantic moment? Do your parents snoop?

The Old Testament is full of stories of kings who started their years on the throne with good intentions, but ended up like their fathers—worshiping idols and forsaking the Lord. One of the most courageous heroes was Josiah who "did what was right in the eyes of the Lord" when as an eight-year-old he became king. Clearly, he developed his own tradition "not turning aside to the right or to the left" (2 Kings 22:2). He publicly confessed that "our fathers have not obeyed" God (v. 13).

Josiah supervised the destruction of the articles made for Baal worship. He killed the pagan priests. He ripped down the Asherah pole from the temple and he tore down the quarters of the male shrine prostitutes. He ended child sacrifice. The Word concludes, "Neither before nor after Josiah was there a king like him who turned to the Lord as he did" (2 Kings 23:25). Why? Because Josiah developed his own traditions.

Traditions are not established or disconnected easily. Old traditions die hard. But if a tradition annoys or even burdens you, it has not served its purpose. You must decide if there is significant value in continuing it. Perhaps it is time for a new tradition.

GUIDELINE NINE: OBEY GOD

What made Josiah successful as a king? He "turned to the Lord . . . with all his heart and with all his soul and with all his strength" (2 Kings 23:25). You will have to do the same.

Today the "chain of command" theory forces the issue of

parental obedience well beyond sound dimensions. If Jesus, for example, had "obeyed" His mother, He would have ended up in a carpenter's shop rather than at Calvary.

What about Jesus' *strong* words, "Do not suppose that I have come to bring peace to the earth. I did not come to bring peace, but a sword. For I have come to turn a man against his father, a daughter against her mother" (Matt. 10:34-35). "Anyone who loves his father or mother more than Me is not worthy of Me. . . . Anyone who does not take up his cross and follow Me is not worthy of Me" (vv. 37-38).

There were people in the early church who were so busy with ministry that they didn't take time to adequately care for their own parents. Paul said that a widow should be cared for by children or grandchildren. "These should learn first of all to put their religion into practice by caring for their own family and so repaying their parents and grandparents, for this is pleasing to God" (1 Tim. 5:4).

Luther Rice provided a model. He grew up in the early 1800s on a Massachusetts farm. It was then expected that the youngest son would remain at home and help the father farm. Yet, Rice had dreams. After his conversion, he held prayer meetings in his home; his parents refused to attend.

Luther eventually sold part of his land to go to college. There he felt a call to the mission field. At that time there were no American-born missionaries. Soon he discovered that the Congregationalists were sending out candidates. In just six days he raised his support money.

On February 6, 1812, in his commissioning service, Rice was asked, "Are you resolved to do everything, *to part with everything,* to submit to everything, to forward this glorious design of filling the earth with the knowledge of the Lord?"[5]

Consider the results of his obedience. Rice created an American consciousness for missions. While one congregation could not support a missionary, Rice believed that if churches would contribute to a fund, as a group they could support a missionary. Rice rode from hamlet to hamlet, selling his missions strategy. In one twelve-month period, he rode 6,600 miles by horseback and collected $4,000.

Rice helped form the Triennial Convention of Baptists, the forerunner of today's Southern Baptist Convention.

Rice lobbied for an educated clergy in a day when Baptist ministers were self-taught. He founded George Washington University in Washington, D.C., to train ministers and other professionals. Later he helped establish other denominational colleges.

He rebutted the Anti-Missions contingent among Baptists who argued that God would save all that needed to be saved.[6]

Luther Rice could have caved in to his father's wishes and remained a New England farmer. But he *chose* to obey God and literally turned the world upside down. Rice helped shape the American commitment to foreign missions.

Am I saying that you too will be a dynamic spiritual leader? I believe that your obedience has consequences—even eternal ones.

CONCLUSION

Building an adult relationship with your parents does not happen overnight. It may require a lifetime of work, three steps forward, two steps backward.

Building an adult relationship with your parents can be painful, lonely, and disheartening. However, it is good preparation for building good relationships with in-laws if and when you marry. And it prepares you for the eventual responsibilities of aging parents.

Tragically, too many single adults have remained children, modern-day Peter Pans, who prefer not to grow up. They prefer the safe, warm cocoon of their parents' love.

Coming to terms with your parents is part of the agenda of adulthood.

COMING TO TERMS WITH YOUR WORK
5

I have never met anyone who has said, "Oh, I just love First and Second Chronicles!"

I've never heard anyone proof-text from either book or use a verse from either book to encourage. Yet, *all* Scripture is "useful for teaching, rebuking, correcting and training in righteousness, so that the man of God may be thoroughly equipped for every good work" (2 Tim. 3:16-17).

In 1 Chronicles we find a list of names of Levite priests—priest after priest, name after name. Hardly anything to rebuke or correct with. Then in 1 Chronicles 4 something strange happens. Two verses are squeezed in between the list, like mortar between bricks:

> Jabez was more honorable than his brothers. His mother had named him Jabez, saying "I gave birth to him in pain." Jabez cried out to the God of Israel, "Oh that You would bless me and enlarge my territory! Let Your hand be with me, and keep me from harm so that I will be free from pain." And God granted his request (1 Chron. 4:9-10).

Then the writer resumed the listing of names: "Kelub, Shuhah's brother, was the father of Mehir, who was. . . . "

It's a mystery passage—a diamond in the rough waiting to be cut into a gemstone.

Sometimes parents give their children funny names. One-time Texas Governor Hogg had a daughter named Ima. No wonder she remained single. Would you want to date Ima Hogg? (Legend has it that she had a sister named Ura, but that is a myth.)

During her father's term, Ima served as his social secretary. Over the years she developed an incredible art collection which she donated to the state of Texas. She overcame her name.

As a child I hated my middle name, Ivan, though I had been named for my grandfather. Perhaps it was the teasing on the playground: "Ivan the Terrible," etc. Yet when my grandfather died and his only other namesake was killed, suddenly there were no more Ivans in the family. Besides, I had moved to San Diego and there were already twenty-seven *Harold Smiths* in the telephone book. So I became Harold *Ivan* Smith.

Names have strange powers. In some countries parents do not name their children at birth. They take time to study the child's personality so that the name is appropriate.

Can you imagine a mother naming her child with a word synonymous to pain: *Jabez*? It would be like a mother naming a child *Bill* because the hospital bill was so large. Jabez must have endured some teasing for his name.

Several times in the Old Testament, at significant junctures in people's lives, they received new names. Jacob became Israel; Sarai became Sarah; Abram became Abraham. Once Jabez had grown to adulthood, he could have asked God to change his name. Instead, he asked for a change of attitude through his prayer.

APPEALING FOR A BLESSING

"Oh that You would wonderfully bless me" (1 Chron. 4:9, TLB). Jabez's first prayer request was a petition for blessing. Unfortunately, we cannot reconstruct his inference. Was it:

Oh that YOU would wonderfully bless me!

Oh that You would wonderfully bless ME!

The second way smacks of arrogance (though it is typical of

the prayers of some of today's single adults, especially those locked in First-Person Singular thinking).

Remarkably, Jabez chose to ask God to bless him in spite of his name. Jabez's action reminds us that God is our source. It's easy to think of our employer as our source. No wonder we worry so much about our jobs. Yet, in actuality, our employer is merely a conduit through which God operates.

Some single adults have a narrow understanding of "bless." They reason they could be blessed by finding their Prince or Princess Charming.

Others see blessing in light of trinkets and loot. The prosperity gospel has made big inroads into mainstream evangelical thinking. Some insist, "Name it and CLAIM it, brother!" Others go a step further and color in the blanks. "If God wants you driving a Cadillac, you just need to tell Him what color you prefer."

Many singles have latched onto this concept. "You want a mate, Honey? Just ask!" Though they add, "no good thing does He withhold," generally they fail to quote the entire verse—"*from those whose walk is blameless*" (Ps. 84:11).

The prosperity gospel is similar to pyramid thinking. It generally works for those who got in first and early. They *do* drive the Cadillacs and sport giant pinky diamond rings. They have the trinkets because the people at the bottom of the pyramid supply the cash to buy the trinkets.

God's Word will work *anywhere*. Yet in Haiti you can find a lot of single adults starving. Why? The prosperity gospel works best in *rich* nations.

What is God's response to a proper request? There is nothing wrong with you repeating Jabez's prayer, verbatim. But how will God respond? The first response is found in 1 John 5:14, "This is the assurance we have in approaching God: That if we ask anything according to His will, He hears us." Read that again. It's easy for singles to do a "Reader's Digest" edit of that verse and eliminate the key thought "according to *His* will."

What is assurance? There were times, as a child, when I approached my dad for money for a candy bar or a model airplane. Generally, I felt more "assurance" asking *after* a payday than before a payday. Fortunately, God has no paydays. John says our assurance is found in asking in God's name and His will.

Single adults must not forget that we are children of the Heavenly Father. We must emphasize the Giver rather than any gift. Clearly, God wants to give His children "good gifts," but within His will.

What is a blessed single adult?

Blessed singles have their priorities clear. Our priorities are framed not on marriage but on seeking FIRST the kingdom (Matt. 6:33). "Seek ye first the kingdom of God and His righteousness." Well, so far, so good. And "all these things shall be added unto you" (KJV).

Can we really believe that? Or do we want to be the ones to define "these things"? Is a diamond ring to be part of the package? Can a "blessed" adult be one who leaves no stone unturned in his or her search for a mate?

Blessed single adults are patient. I would paraphrase the psalmist— "Blessed is the single who bringeth forth his fruit in his season; his leaf shall not wither and whatsoever he does, shall prosper" (1:3). Some single adults have to conclude, "This isn't my season to be married."

But other single adults insist, "My schedule! My time frame, if you don't mind." One single wrote to me saying, "It may be a 'season in my life' for you, but it's a long, cold winter for me!"

Blessed singles are kind and merciful (Matt. 5:7). A businessman, facing bankruptcy, went to see Andrew Carnegie. The bank was threatening immediate foreclosure and Carnegie was his last hope to save his name and business. After he had pleaded with the magnate, Carnegie walked him to the door. He put his hand on the man's shoulder and said, "Well, I just believe everything is going to work out. I've got confidence in you."

Carnegie did not loan the man the money. The man was devastated. However, the banker who owned his notes overheard Carnegie's confidence in the man. "If Carnegie believes in him, so can I."

The loans were reissued and the man prospered. Carnegie used his jaw to help another, though not in the way the needy man anticipated. Be open to surprises.

APPEALING FOR HELP

The second dimension of Jabez's prayer is, "Oh, that You would enlarge my territory." Or "that You would help me in my work" (TLB).

I taught for four years in a ghetto school. I hated it. I grew to hate Sunday afternoons because they reminded me that soon it would be time to go back to the school. Part of my dilemma was *my* poor attitude toward my work.

Are you aware that God is interested in your vocation? Whether you are a truck driver, a nurse, or a banker. Whatever you do, God is interested in that job. Your job is a way to reflect God's glory. Katherine Lackman explained:

> As I see it, I'm required to do my work, whatever it is, as diligently and caringly as Jesus would have done the same job had He chosen my profession for a while. I often fail in that diligence and must ask for forgiveness. But my work is still to God's glory and is an offering to Him, and through my diligence and my love (for my work) I have a chance to show something of Christ.[1]

Part of our problem is the confusion over distinctions between the laity and the clergy. Many have embraced the notion that the clergy is somehow exalted over the laity. But God does not have two classes of servants. Nor does He call those He loves the most to the clergy. A lay person is just as called as an ordained minister. In fact, the early church prospered without professional leadership. There were no seminaries for the early Christians. Rather, those individuals made the most of their opportunities to share the Good News.

Think about that phrase from the Lord's Prayer, "Give us each day our daily bread" (Luke 11:3). It is often hard for American singles to understand that, let alone pray for bimonthly or monthly bread. Yet, in many world areas, Christians must rely on God to provide their daily needs.

Whatever your job or profession, it is a means of gathering resources to build God's kingdom. Some of those hours when you hate your job, do you remember that a portion of that money—made that hour or that day—will find its way into mission programs halfway across the world? Or do you think of those unemployed people who would like to have your job?

Our work provides resources to answer the prayers of others. It's too easy to pray, "O Lord, help Mary Jones. You know that she's a single parent and her ex is a bona fide lowlife and is behind six months in alimony and child support." It's easy to get our "stained-glass voices" raised to a high pitch and our cadence flowing so that others are "Amening." Sometimes, however, God interrupts: "Why don't *you* do something about the needs of Mary Jones?"

The temptation is to turn up the volume on our prayer. As if God didn't hear us the first time.

Many single adults have the ability to answer their own prayers and the prayers of others. That is why God has chosen to bless them. Paul reminded the Corinthians in light of the needs of the saints in Jerusalem, "Your plenty will supply what they need" (2 Cor. 8:14). My "plenty"?

Joan wanted to give money to a special missionary project at the church, but there wasn't enough left over each week. However, in faith, she signed the pledge card and asked God to open the doors so that she could fulfill her pledge. She was not surprised when her boss asked her to work overtime. The overtime did not supply money for Joan's luxury list, but it supplied the need.

American single adults have a unique opportunity to bless others. Paul said, "God loves a cheerful giver" (2 Cor. 9:17). My friend Mike Murdock adds, "But He'll take from a grouch." That verse doesn't mean that God hates a reluctant giver. But "God loves" or delights in cheerful giving.

Have you considered that you are God's ambassador at your workplace? God wants to use you as a witness to people who desperately need to *see* the Gospel. That's why our work ethic and performance are so important. Are you perceived as lazy? You may read your *King James* at your desk as a "witness," but laziness contradicts it.

Some of you may protest, "You don't know what it's like to work in my office. There's so much smoke and foul talk. I can't even see my typewriter some days." Or, "This woman next to me is a Canaanite, for sure. She's so promiscuous and so are all the men." Sometimes single adults ask, "Would you pray that I can find a new job?"

Often we need to ask God to give us a "change of attitude" rather than a change of circumstances. While it won't make the cigarette smoking any less offensive, a new attitude will help us to care for the person who happens to be a smoker.

Another facet of this is to recognize the value of all honest work. Many career-minded singles have become overly impressed with their resumés and ladder-climbing. Their first question is usually "What do you do?" rather than "How do you do?"

So what if a single adult is a cook at McDonald's? I want to know if he is a *good* cook. Does he take pride in what he does?

Admittedly, not everyone can be upwardly mobile. New York City garbage collectors earn more than many college professors. Yet, obviously the professors have more status. So the garbage collectors have turned to unions to gain respect. Similarly, single adults may buy the trinkets and status symbols of singledom to compensate for their low job status or lack of a wedding ring.

Another danger is that single adults easily become workaholics. It is easy to compensate for a poor social life by putting in more hours on the job. After all, the early bird (and the hard-working bird) gets the worm (bonus/promotion).

How many single adults have poured themselves into their jobs and have gained status, prestige, promotions, and newsletter write-ups? How many are far ahead of their peer pack, yet run with one eye back over their shoulder? How many are troubled by the question, "Is it worth it?"

Joseph Conrad observed, "I don't like work—no man does—but I like what is in work—the chance to find yourself."[2]

AN APPEAL FOR ACCOMPANYING

One reason many people like work is for the work intimacy. Pulling together to make, build, or maintain something that is greater than themselves. I'd like to attend a ship launching. A thousand different crafts have been necessary to build a nuclear aircraft carrier or submarine. Many people have worked together as a team to accomplish this task.

What makes it worth the long hours? According to John Ruskin, three factors cause people to be happy in their work. "They must be fit for it. They must not do too much of it. And they must have a sense of success in it."[3]

Our work leads to the third dimension of Jabez's prayer: "Oh, that You would be with me *in all that I do.*" Jesus is anxious to be Lord of every dimension of our lives: body, mind, soul, and muscles.

God said, "Six days you shall labor and do all your work, but the seventh day is a Sabbath to the Lord your God. On it you shall not do any work" (Ex. 20:9-10). Admittedly, in an urban-technological society like ours, that is difficult. Maybe it was easier when Sunday was a national "day of rest."

Too many single adults want their schedules to be so busy that there is not a moment of rest or reflection. How many return from a vacation exhausted? How many take recreation too seriously?

Indeed, some want single adult ministries to fill up every vacant moment. But God asks single adults to "be still, and know that I am God" to find those times of rest (Ps. 46:10, KJV). I am struck by the number of times that Scripture reports that Jesus "got away." For example, after He had fed the 5,000 He "went up into the hills *by Himself* to pray" (Matt. 14:23).

Single adults today need time to be alone. Time to hear our heartbeat. Time to hear God. Time to wait. If only we could invite God to be part of "all that we do." The writer of

Ecclesiastes noted:

> I realized that it is good and proper for a man to eat and drink, and to find satisfaction in his toilsome labor under the sun during the few days of life God has given him—for this is his lot. Moreover, when God gives any man wealth and possessions, and enables him to enjoy them, to accept his lot and be happy in his work—this is a gift of God. He seldom reflects on the days of his life, because God keeps him occupied with gladness of heart (Ecc. 5:18-20).

God wants to accompany us through our singleness. He will guide those He accompanies. Isaiah noted, "The Lord will guide you continually, and satisfy you with all good things, and keep you healthy too" (58:11 TLB).

God is as concerned about the other sixteen hours of the day as the eight hours we spend on the job.

APPEAL FOR KEEPING

Jabez concluded his petition with an appeal, "Keep me from all harm so that I will be free from pain." We are so sensitive to evil and disaster. Newspapers, TV, and radio keep us informed of disasters in places we cannot pronounce.

But if something terrible could happen there, it could happen *here*. In my zip code! Some parents have 11 P.M. check-up calls to their single adult sons or daughters. "Just wanted to see if you were all right." One mother confessed, "I won't have a night of sleep until my daughter gets married."

Single adults need to remember that God is in control. He will never lead us where His grace cannot keep us.

I think of those heroic adults who went to the foremost corners of the globe as missionaries in the late 1880s. I think of Lottie Moon, notifying two warring tribes that at a certain hour she would be passing through their battlefield. Sure enough, the fighting stopped until she had safely passed through the area; then it resumed.[4]

I think of Gladys Aylward, a single missionary in China. When the Japanese invaded in 1940, she heroically led 100 children through the mountains to safety.[5]

These women and hundreds like them saw risk as part of their work. In order to do the tasks to which they felt called, they had to rely on the Lord for protection.

Often single adults forget that this is our Father's world. The Word instructs us, "Have no fear of sudden disaster." Sure, awful things do happen in this world. But Paul asked, "Who (or what) shall separate us from the love of Christ?" (Rom. 8:35) His answer—*nothing!*

CONCLUSION

Thomas Carlyle said, "Blessed is he who has found his work; let him ask no other blessedness."[6] I dare you to consider praying Jabez's prayer. The God who never changes is anxious to be as gracious and generous with you as He was to Jabez. The Scripture concludes, "And God granted his request" (1 Chron. 4:10).

You—regardless of the reason for your singleness—can pray Jabez's prayer. The Proverbs encourage: "Trust in the Lord with all your heart and lean not unto your own understanding; *in all your ways* acknowledge Him and He will make your paths straight" (Prov. 3:5-6).

God longs to help you in your work. To be with you in all that you do. To keep you safe. This season—however long in duration—can be an opportunity to grow, to stretch, to become all that God desires you to be.

Coming to terms with the agenda of life means coming to terms with your work.

QUESTIONS

1. How do I want work to fit into my life? Do I like my hours? Do I have adequate time for my personal life? For church activities?

2. How much money do I really need? How much money do I want?

3. What skills do I like to use? Which ones do I hate to use?

4. How would I rate my job performance?

5. Does my job offer a sufficient range of activity and human contact?

6. Am I comfortable with the level of responsibility and autonomy I have? Do I have too much or too little supervision?

7. Am I working to my full potential? If not, why not?

8. Does my job provide me with a sense of self-esteem?

9. Do I have a sense that I am influencing what goes on around me?

10. What goals did I begin with? Have I drifted away from those goals?

11. Am I happy?[7]

12. How would Jesus do my job?

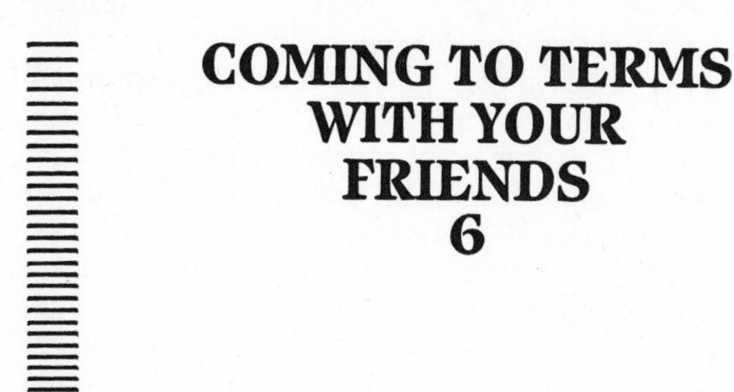

COMING TO TERMS WITH YOUR FRIENDS 6

"No more close friends! Ever!" The attractive young woman's sharp outburst surprised me. "All I do is give bridal showers."

Have you had a friendship strangled by such a possessive overtone? Have you had to "divorce" a friendship? Did the relationship that was going to be so wonderful unravel as the friend's "true" personality became evident? For others, relationships have become DMZ's or a harbor for two ships passing in the night.

Single relationships may be the most difficult to maintain. What can be rewarding and beneficial can also be frustrating.

WHY DO WE NEED FRIENDS ANYWAY?

Art Carey has suggested that friends are sought for three principal reasons: companionship, structure, and stability or security.[1] I'd like to add five other reasons.

1. *Companionship.* After all, doesn't Genesis 2:18 say, "It is not good for the [single] to be alone"? A friend is someone to do things with, unless he or she is into heavy dating. Then as your brother or sister used to remind you, "Two's company; three's a crowd!"

2. *Structure.* Some single adults form relationships to

share habits. A friend to eat breakfast with on Saturday mornings, then go shopping. A friend with whom you can cruise K-Mart on Friday nights for the "blue light specials." When likes and dislikes are similar (or tolerable), a friend is someone with whom you can share certain activities and often yourself (thoughts/moods/fears). In fact, a good friendship can compensate for a lack of dating.

3. *Security.* One advantage of being single is that you can have friendships with members of either sex that might threaten a mate. A friend offers emotional security by "being there" for those times of crisis your mother predicted would happen.

4. *Loneliness.* It's hard to come home to nothing but four walls. A friend adds to the landscape of our lives. That way you don't have to walk into Burger Doodle alone. Or you have someone to sit with at church.

The acquisition of friends can make the single life easier. However, it will be advantageous to find a friend whose "average dating frequency" is compatible with yours. The two of you can become a "tag team" or dynamic duo.

5. *Intimacy.* It's a cold, cruel world out there. Certainly there is a dimension of our lives in which we need intimacy: someone to be there. Someone who understands and can translate with a minimum of difficulty those "black and blue traumas of ordinary living." Someone who in Eugene Kennedy's words, catches "the faintest echo of our inner wounds" and fears. Who knows our "great secrets and small shames."[2]

This "someone" understands our struggles and our defeats, as well as our longings. This "someone" nods or mutters, at appropriate and sometimes inappropriate moments, "I know what you mean." This "someone" listens to our stories, *again.*

Researchers at Harvard have studied the lives of several hundred female "superachievers." One fascinating detail is that many had lifelong companions. Mary Williams Dewson, a politician, lived with Marg Porter; Gordon Hamilton (a woman), a social worker who linked medicine with social work, lived with Anna Kempshall. Winifred Louise Ward, a children's theater innovator, lived with Hazel Eastman for fifty years. Mabel Willebradt, nicknamed "first lady of the law," lived with Louise Stanley, a pioneer in home economics education.[3]

Some relationships were called "Boston marriages." Many lifelong relationships developed between friends who had attended Eastern women's colleges. Though there is a subtle double standard, certainly nothing in the term "Boston marriage" implies homosexual preference.

When I moved into my predominantly Jewish neighborhood, one of the older neighbors stared at me as I carried in boxes.

"And just how many children are you bringing into our quiet neighborhood?" she demanded in thick Americanized Yiddish.

"None," I shrugged.

"Such a shame! These career women. They wait too late to have the babies."

"No," I interrupted her lament. "I'm not married."

I got a quick, head to toe once-over that suggested, *You look old enough to be married.* Then she chuckled, "Maybe you are a smart boy, after all. Get a nice house like this . . . you'll get a better girl."

There are seven distinct barriers which act to prevent good relationships.

BARRIERS TO GOOD RELATIONSHIPS

1. *Pettiness.* If you don't have to have a friend but you want to have one, it's easy to be picky. Some single adults are "old-maidish" (whether male or female) about their possessions. Some friendships have been strained over "who paid last time" or "We always eat where *you* want to eat!"

2. *Selfishness.* Suppose your friend asks to use or borrow something of yours. There are certain ways of saying yes ("I suppose it would be all right") that discourage future requests. The other alternative is to buy cheap so that your friends won't want to borrow from you.

It is so easy as a single adult to become so self-focused that selfishness becomes a by-product. Everything must focus on me: *my* needs, *my* schedule, *my* preferences.

3. *Vast economic differences.* Suppose you're going out to eat. Where do you go—Burger King or Steak and Ale? Sometimes choosing a place, within an acceptable price range, can be frustrating.

Some single adults use material possessions as barometers of their self-worth. They think, *I am what I drive or wear or own.* Some singles become covetous or even jealous and that sabotages potential friendships.

4. *Vast moral differences.* It will be difficult for you to walk "the straight and narrow" if you have bona fide Philistine friends. For example, some single adults have differing standards on wine. Others drink an occasional or social beer. So will you tag along with the gang after work to "happy hour" and sip your ginger ale?

It's easy for us to adopt the standards of the world gradually, piecemeal, through accommodation and rationalization.

5. *Vast educational differences.* Education, particularly higher education, influences and alters opinions and attitudes. Some singles are cerebral: they like to read; they like quiet times; they prefer Brahms or Bach.

For others, the comic strip "Cathy" is a taxing intellectual exercise. While cerebral singles are struggling through some great book, really extracting nourishment for their minds, their friends might be devouring a steamy romance novel.

So what do they talk about? Who's going to win the pennant? The latest automobile design? It is essential for friends to talk about more than casual or surface issues.

6. *Dating.* The heartbreak of singlehood is dating. How many of us feel left out?

Suppose you and your friend have gone to K-Mart on Friday nights for the last five years. You call to see what time to "drop by," but she responds that she has a date.

"What?" you scold. "But we *always* go to K-Mart on Friday nights!"

The more your friends date, the less time they have for you. And it's easy to feel neglected when you're sitting home burping your Tupperware or watching TV reruns.

7. *Stress.* What if you acquire a friend who thrives on crises? Who cannot handle stress of any kind? Who's always calling and asking, "What am I gonna do?"

Maintenance can be one-sided. If one friend is continually called upon to "shore-up" the sagging ego or spirits of the other, the friendship will be jeopardized. Some singles want friends to be surrogate mothers or fathers. That's an impossible role for a friend to fill.

Yet there are nutrients which nourish a friendship and help it become a "soul mate" relationship, as existed between David and Jonathan. Their relationship offers nine helpful principles of friendship.

PRINCIPLES OF A GOOD FRIENDSHIP

1. *A good friend attracts.* "Jonathan became one in spirit with David, and he loved him as himself" (1 Sam. 18:1). Good relationships do not just coincidentally happen. All develop and require a lot of time, patience, and energy.

As we meet single adults, we often test their potential for friendship. Would this person make a good friend? The best friendships have formed over a period of time. Few instant relationships last long.

Jonathan apparently cared for David *before* he actually met him. There is no indication that they knew each other. Sometimes we plant a friend-seed, saying in essence, "If you ever need a friend. . . ." Sometimes, we send out subtle smoke signals, afraid of rejection. Clearly, as we converse, we make impressions which we will later scrutinize. "Hmm . . . might make a good friend, down the road."

2. *A good friend commits.* "And Jonathan made a covenant with David because he loved him as himself" (1 Sam. 18:3). Often single adults invest cautiously in a friendship because we have been burned in previous relationships. Besides he or she might get married or transferred, so why overly invest? Yet that caution breeds loneliness and isolation.

This particular biblical passage is significant. Singles, especially men, are afraid to commit themselves to nourishing a covenantal relationship with another single. What would people think? Herb Goldberg identified five stages in relationship formation:

Stage One	Acquaintance phase	Face/name recognition.
Stage Two	Manipulative phase	"He can get it for me wholesale" or "Scratch my back; I'll scratch yours."
Stage Three	Companion phase	Focus on activities or doing things "together."
Stage Four	Friend phase	Enough interaction to foster a friendship.
Stage Five	Buddy phase	Has passed a test or threat.[4]

Buddyships are important. Generally, they are formed in light of a mutual danger—for example, in wartime. That's why men from World War II still gather for reunions four decades later.

The healthiest relationships survive and thrive when *both* friends honor each other. You don't conceal something that is bothering you. You cautiously use the manacing "you" vocabulary. You don't cancel a meal or racquetball game because you got a date with Miss Farm Bureau or a Tom Selleck lookalike. You don't always insist on your rights.

3. *A good friend gives.* "Jonathan took off the robe he was wearing and gave it to David, along with his tunic, and even his sword, his bow, and his belt" (1 Sam. 18:4). Someone has said that marriage is a 50/50 proposition. Well, sometimes in marriage it has to be 90/10. The same is true in good friendships.

A vulnerability existed between these two men. Jonathan, though royalty, gave to a peasant on a level that David could not reciprocate. Some relationships exist on a balance: you give so much, *then* (and only then) I will give so much. The relationship survives as long as the balance is even.

Earlier, Jonathan's father, Saul, had tried to give David his tunic and his coat of armor and a bronze helmet. David responded, "I cannot go in these because I am not used to them" (1 Sam. 17:39).

Now, David accepts similar gifts from Saul's son. These were significant, personal gifts. Jonathan was not attempting to manipulate David with his gifts. He didn't buy the relationship.

Additionally, as a result of Jonathan's giving, a nakedness developed—a stripping, both physical and psychological. David accepted these gifts though he could not reciprocate. In our friendships some gifts have no dollar value. Friends can always give:

- encouragement
- advice
- counsel
- time
- space

Giving is a basic element in a thriving relationship. There are no scales to keep balanced: one good deed to match your good deed. No IOUs. A relationship can bog down in mathematical calculations when one friend is always trying to keep the scales balanced.

4. *A good friend shares.* "Jonathan was very fond of David and warned him" (1 Sam. 19:1-2). Jonathan's heroic action meant that he ignored his own interests. Saul had told Jonathan and "all the attendants" to kill David. Jonathan chose to disclose that order to David. He said, "I'll speak to him (Saul) about you and will tell you what I find out." Talk about a Deep Throat in the palace. The heir apparent was the leak.

Good friends share the good, the bad, *and* the ugly. Sometimes, we like people to tell us what we want to hear. We even hint broadly at what we would like for them to say.

But a good friend tells us, at times, tactfully, things that we may not want to hear. Sometimes a friend may have to risk the friendship or our anger. Tact always "greases" the pan for such comments and time smoothes ruffled feathers.

5. *A good friend defends.* "Jonathan spoke well of David to

Saul his father . . . he has not wronged you" (1 Sam. 19:4). Jonathan ignored his own vested interest. He could have insisted, "This is between David and my father."

Indeed, this is one consequence of the lack of commitment in relationships and friendships. In conversations, rarely do we strongly defend a friend. However, in your friendship you may have discovered a side of your friend that others have not seen. A good friend is a brother or ally.

One way to defend our friendships is by never disclosing information to third parties that might hurt or threaten the relationship. Sometimes you filter what your friend has revealed to you in a guarded moment.

Jonathan chose to defend *the person,* not the relationship. As we do the same, sometimes we must take on some antagonism. Look what Saul bellowed: "You son of a perverse and rebellious woman!" (20:30)

That's a hostile accusation. Saul is on the verge of suggesting that David and Jonathan are homosexually involved. But Jonathan stands his ground and guards his friendship.

6. *A good friend confronts.* "David . . . went to Jonathan and asked, 'What have I done? What is my crime? How have I wronged your father that he is trying to take my life?' " (1 Sam. 20:1)

Have you ever sensed a tiff and asked, "Is anything wrong?"

"*Wrong*? What makes you think anything is *wrong*?"

The verbal punctuation tells you that something is definitely wrong. In some friendships you can learn to translate the silence by moods or even by body English to conclude, *there's a problem.*

Some of us take the philosophical approach and ignore the problem, hoping it will go away. Unfortunately, as a result of the avoidance, the problem usually gets worse.

Sometimes, simple things sour a relationship. We get so self-confident at translating nonverbal clues that we ultimately misinterpret an action or statement. When Jonathan responded, "Never!" David immediately rejected his denial. "Your father knows very well that I have found favor in your eyes"

(1 Sam. 20:3). Jonathan could not deny David's statement.

Because David loved Jonathan, he could not let him ignore the implications of Saul's conduct. But David had his facts straight before he confronted Jonathan.

You cannot let things slide. Do you care enough to confront?

7. *A good friend sacrifices.* "Jonathan said to David, 'Whatever you want me to do, I'll do for you'" (20:4). If there has to be a winner, there has to be a loser. It may be in simple things you learn to sacrifice or *choose* to sacrifice. Can you sacrifice the place to eat or the time that would be most convenient for you? The small sacrifices pave the way for the larger ones.

Too many friends complain, "There's only one way of doing things—my friend's way!" What a sad commentary.

You can sacrifice without being a doormat or feeling used or manipulated. Sacrifice is part of all thriving relationships.

8. *A good friend invests emotion.* "David got up from the south side of the stone and bowed down before Jonathan three times, with his face to the ground. Then they kissed each other and wept together—but David wept the most" (1 Sam. 20:41).

Some of us do not want to emotionally invest in friendships because so many relationships are temporary. But riskless relationships are sterile. No investment and no risk means no dividend.

One in five Americans moves each year; the average among single adults may be higher. Admittedly, it hurts when friends move away. If their "ship comes in" before yours does. If they get a promotion into another social set and you remain behind. To start over again means being vulnerable and risking.

It's often hard for males to say, "I'm going to miss *you!*" So we mumble something. However, this verse shows that emotions are masculine but not necessarily equal.

There is real grief when a friend "moves on" emotionally or physically. Ben Patterson shared this example:

> I went through what amounted to two broken engagements over a five-year period—with the same girl. When it was all over, forever, and we knew it, I went to visit a close friend who had been intimately acquainted with the details of everything that had happened during that painful and stormy period of my life. I was numb and tired of hurting. We talked for a while and when I got up to leave he suggested that we pray together. I prayed first and then waited for him to begin. Nothing came for a long time. I was about to ask what was wrong when I heard something. It was a sob. Cliff was weeping for me when I could no longer weep for myself. There have been few times in my life when I have felt as comforted. He was a little bit of the Holy Spirit to me at that moment.[5]

What an incredible and sensitive friend!

9. *A good friend supports.* "Saul's son Jonathan went to David at Horesh and helped him find strength in God" (1 Sam. 23:16). That phrase "helped him find strength in God" overwhelms me. The son of the source of David's problem was his tear-catcher.

When life caves in—you will need a friend. It will help if the foundations have already been laid. In such moments, there is an intimacy of silence—of shared thoughts that do not have to be put into words.

Moreover, we are to be spiritual helpmates as well as friends. A real friend helps us find strength in God. That is a great test: Does this person help me find strength?

Ultimately, we should evaluate friendships by asking, "Have I grown spiritually since ________ became my friend?" Or, "Am I closer or farther from the Lord because of ________?"

WHY ARE FRIENDSHIPS SO IMPORTANT?

Friendships are mirrors in which we see our shallowness, our imperfections, our inadequacies, our self-focus. Friendships are emotional bootcamps to help us mature. To help us deal with the more complex friendship of a mate.

Friendships prevent premature marriages. How many marriages have resulted because of inadequate friendships? How many people have pushed the romance button from "simmer" to "hot" because their best friend got married and they didn't want to be alone?

We are not called to be emotional lone rangers. The Bible mentions *twos:* Paul, though unmarried, did not wander around solo. He had special relationships with Silas, Barnabas, Timothy, John Mark, and Luke. In fact, we see a glimpse into Paul's need for intimacy as he pleads with Timothy, "Do your best to come to me *quickly,* for Demas . . . has deserted me. . . . Only Luke is with me" (2 Tim. 4:9-11).

We are a people designed for others. If Jesus, the most psychologically whole person, needed others, how much more do we?

Let's take a look at Jesus' friendships.

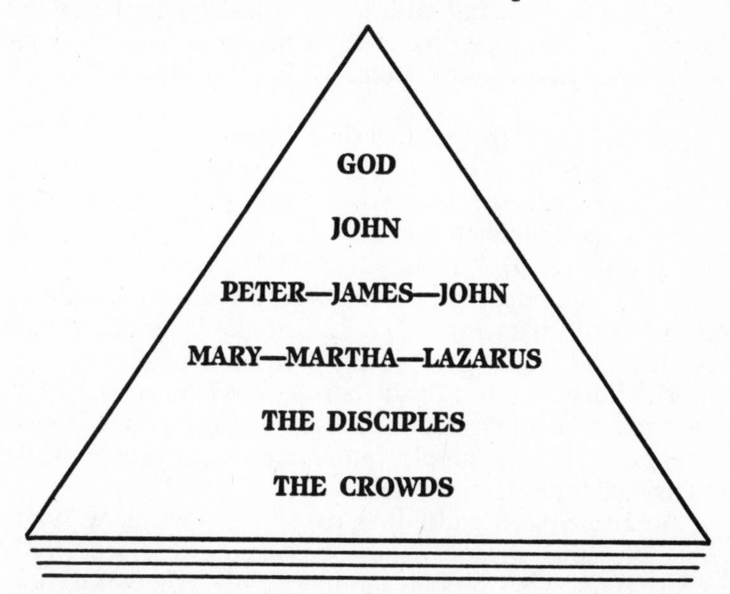

At the bottom—or at the widest point—He had the crowds. Highly impersonal. Most centered on Jesus meeting *their* needs. Next came the disciples. But even they argued about who would be seated next to Him in the coming kingdom.

Then came that special relationship with Mary, Martha, and Lazarus. Jesus often enjoyed their home and hospitality. It once sparked conflict between the sisters. When Lazarus was ill, the sisters sent for Jesus: "Lord, the one *You love* is sick" (John 11:3). Later their annoyance is evident when Jesus arrived after Lazarus' death. "Lord, if You had been here, my brother would not have died" (John 11:21, 32). Jesus was moved by Mary's tears (v. 33). Jesus recognized the value of friendships.

But look at the next level. Out of the disciples, Jesus chose three: Peter, James, and John. At significant moments (at His transfiguration and in the Garden of Gethsemane), they were present.

Then there is the relationship with John. Out of the twelve, John was the one with whom Jesus had developed the closest friendship. Five times John is mentioned as "the disciple (or one) Jesus loved" (John 13:23; 19:26; 20:2; 21:7; 21:20).

The relationship was not fully understood, particularly by Peter. When Jesus warned Peter of the kind of death Peter would face, "Peter turned and saw that the disciple whom *Jesus loved* was following them. . . . 'Lord,'" Peter demanded, "'what about him?'" (John 21:20-21)

Jesus responded, "If I want him to remain alive until I return, what is that to you?" (v. 22) Moreover, to this trusted disciple-friend, Jesus gave custody of his mother.

The Jonathan/David and Jesus/John relationships frighten most of us. I would not want you to misinterpret my intent in mentioning them. Simply, both indicate that people can be selective in forming friendships.

An authentic friendship is risky. Yet how many single adults have that shallow sense of isolation, that ache for a friendship that goes beyond the surface—but they stop short of giving big chunks of themselves to develop such a relationship? Sidney Jourard explained why we avoid such relationships. "We're afraid that if someone knows where to put the balm to heal us, they'll know where to drop the bomb to destroy us."[6]

> The chief risk lies in letting other people know how one has experienced the events impinging on one's life. All that other people can ever see of an individual is the expurgated version he discloses through his action. A man's public utterances are often radically different from what he authentically feels and believes. Many of us dread to be known by others as intimately as we know ourselves because we would be divorced, fired, imprisoned, or shot.[7]

TERMINATIONS

Sometimes, relationships must be terminated. In those cases, it is important to reject the relationship rather than the person. Four factors kill good friendships.

Unexpressed expectations. "I wish he or she would. . . ." These feelings are generally expressed to a third party rather than to the friend.

Unexpressed disappointments. "I wish he or she had. . . ." Sometimes our struggle with a current friendship is influenced by unfinished business from previous ones.

Unexpressed comparisons. "I wish he or she was more like. . . ." Ah, but he's not.

Unexpressed motivations. "I thought he could get it for me wholesale." Too many friendships are initiated and then evaluated on the basis of "what's in it for me."

CONCLUSION

David and Jonathan had a unique same-sex relationship. Can you relate to the deep shattering sense of loss David expressed after Jonathan's death?

> How the mighty have fallen in battle! Jonathan lies slain on your heights. I grieve for you, Jonathan my brother; you were very dear to me. Your love for me was wonderful, more wonderful than that of women (2 Sam. 1:25-26).

Fortunately, David had felt sufficiently free to express his strong emotion to Jonathan *before* his death. But how many single adults are afraid to say to a friend, "You know, I really appreciate you. . . . I really love you"?

How many of us thank God for our friendships?

Friendships are part of the agenda of coming to terms with our singleness.

COMING TO TERMS WITH YOUR ANXIETY 7

A mother and son from a small town in the mountains of Kentucky went to visit relatives in Louisville. On Sunday, they attended a church quite different from the small independent Baptist church they attended at home. When it came time for the sermon, the minister, in a flowing robe, walked to a small staircase that led into a great walnut pulpit. He opened the small gate, stepped through it, then closed the door behind him.

Naturally, this fascinated the eight-year-old. The longer the minister preached, the more animated he became. He waved his arms forcefully and pounded the pulpit. After about twenty-five minutes, the boy tugged his mother's arms. "Mama! What are we gonna do if he gets loose?"

Two words have captured the American public's mind. These two simple words can paralyze a person, a family, a church, or a business: *What if?*

Psychologist Dan Kiley, author of *The Peter Pan Syndrome,* explained, "The textbook definition of *anxiety* says that a person is anxious when he faces a situation in which he must do something but the alternatives appear fruitless."[1] Often he does nothing.

Single adults live in an age of anxiety. I saw a cartoon of a man sitting in front of a TV. The caption was: *Mass mur-*

ders . . . piles of human bones . . . videotapes of torture . . . death chamber . . . to which his roommate yelled: *Is that the news or tonight's made-for-TV movie?*

If you haven't had enough anxiety on your job, thirty minutes of the evening news with Dan Rather or Tom Brokaw should just about meet your saturation level. At 9 P.M. there's "Newsbreak." Then there's the late news—and if you can't go to bed without one more dose, there's Ted Koppel and "Nightline."

Anxiety whispers, "What if *that* happened *here?* Or *to you?*"

Americans love their telethons for assorted diseases and maladies. After all, one in 100,000 Americans have disease X. Since you don't, you should toss a few bucks in the bucket of firemen who are doing their part to raise enough money for research. (I always wonder who's manning the fire hall.)

How do we survive anxiety? Single adults have three tasks: to recognize our anxieties, to understand our anxieties, and to discipline our anxieties.

RECOGNIZING OUR ANXIETIES

What makes you anxious? Death? Illness? Loss of a job? Growing older? Those would be common anxieties. Many single women are anxious about rape or sexual harassment. Some men are anxious about sexual role conflicts or women's assertiveness.

Think about your current anxieties. Ask yourself:

- What are some consequences of my anxiety?
- Am I better off for having this anxiety?
- What nourishes my anxiety?
- How do others deal with this anxiety?
- How would Jesus deal with this anxiety?
- Why do I cling to this anxiety?
- How would I feel without this anxiety?

These are sliding-scaled priorities. Try this paraphrase of 1 Corinthians 13:11: "When I was a child, I was anxious like a child. But when I became an adult, I took on adult anxieties."

Remember your childhood anxieties: such as that your parents would not return from a trip? Or that you had been adopted? Or that your body was not developing on your time schedule? Remember the intense anxiety a teacher could create by saying, "I'm going to call your mother!" Remember the sweat-anxieties of pop quizzes?

Some psychologists believe that many adult anxieties are deeply rooted in childhood.

Then, of course, there are the recently developed anxieties. My grandfather never once worried about his masculinity: he had twelve kids to feed and 300 acres to farm. In those days, a man had two roles: provider and protector. However, his grandsons have to deal with a whole different criteria for masculinity. My grandfather never had to worry about acid rain, dioxide contamination, or asbestos cancer.

Some single adults wrestle with newly intensified anxieties, ones that have long lay dormant. Let an older parent become ill or a son/daughter. What if they do not have adequate insurance? That's intensified anxiety. Most recently divorced or widowed people face this when they are alone and hear all those things that go *Bump!* in the night. There's no one to send to investigate.

However, anxieties can be useful. Anxieties keep us saving money, carrying flashlights in our cars, checking our gas gauges. Anxieties keep us from taking unnecessary risks. Anxieties can be good when they alert us to the potential of danger.

But irrational anxieties destroy, paralyze, and even sabotage. Mack Douglas studied anxiety and concluded:

> 40 percent of an individual's worries are about things that never happen!
>
> 30 percent of an individual's worries relate to things that they can't change!
>
> 12 percent of an individual's worries relate to health!
>
> 10 percent of an individual's worries relate to petty and miscellaneous things.
>
> Thus, only 8 percent of a person's worries are

about real problems; 92 percent are wasted worries.[2]

Paul wrote, "Do not be anxious about anything" (Phil. 4:6). David also learned to trust the Lord in times of trouble: "I sought the Lord, and He answered me; He delivered me from *all* my fears" (Ps. 34:4).

Anxiety can be as devastating to spiritual progress as any sexual temptation. For anxiety takes your reliance off the Lord and puts it on your body, your emotions, your skills, and your resourcefulness.

How do anxieties originate?

Unconscious intrapsychic conflicts. These originate when our psychological needs are out of balance.[3]

Imitation or example. What stimulated your parents' anxiety? My mother was always concerned about our $80 per month mortgage payment. (She'd die if she knew mine.) Maybe your mother was concerned about a proposed strike or her weight. Perhaps after years of being exposed to your parents' fears, you have second or third generation anxiety.

Childhood conflicts. We seldom get far from our childhoods, whether they were good or bad. How many times were you told that you were *bad* or inadequate or too small or too big to do something? Some adults today still hear whispering ghosts or see shadows from the past. Jerome Kagan explained:

> My own image of a life is that of a traveler whose knapsack is slowly filled with doubts, dogma, and *desires during the first dozen years* (italics mine). Each traveler spends the adult years trying to empty the heavy load in the knapsack until he or she can confront the opportunities that are present in each fresh day. Some adults approach this state; most *carry their collection of uncertainties, prejudices,* and frustrated wishes into middle and old age trying to prove what must remain uncertain while raging wildly at ghosts![4]

Present-day situations. If you have spent your Penney's card to its limit, if your Visa and MasterCard are out of control, what happens when you hear that your company is going to lay off employees? And in *your* department?

Or what if you become ill? How many people are afraid to go to the doctor—and yet afraid not to go?

Being anxious about being anxious. Some of us get around the "Happy! Happy! Happy!" Christians who seem to have no problems or have been denying their own feelings so long that they are deluded. Have you ever said, "Everything is going too well"?

Fears of inferiority, poverty, or poor health. Some of our bodies stimulate our anxiety. We create a cycle of anxiety. You feel uptight about the size of your breasts, thighs, or waistline. So you join a health club and pay the $700 initiation fee, most of which you charged on your overweight plastic cards. If you do not go to the club as often as you think you should, you'll feel anxious.

Some singles grew up poor and fear becoming poor. We're paralyzed by thinking *What would I do if I lose my job?* Or *I couldn't change jobs. What would I do to make ends meet?* So, we remain on a job we hate.

Exposure to unfiltered data. One good rumor can create an avalanche of anxiety. "Mr. Jones said *we might* (key words) have to cut back!" becomes, after three repetitions and slight alteration before coffee break, "Mr. Jones said we *are* cutting back!" Soon the story has mushroomed into, "Seven people are getting laid off"—and they're all coming out of your department. Naturally, you become anxious.

Other sources. There are other sources for anxiety such as structure, technology, the behavior of others, and assumptions/values. We like structure and organization in our lives—a sense of "what to expect" or what we can get away with. What happens if you move halfway across the country? What happens if you have to sleep in a different bed tonight?

Tamper with structure and people get uneasy. That is why some single adults get into a routine: Monday night they go to Burger King; Tuesday night they make stovetop lasagna; Wednesday night is McDonald's. They settle into predictable patterns or ruts to avoid anxiety.

Technology, especially the computer, produces anxiety. What would we do without high tech? Yet, do you feel comfortable with your computer skills? Automation stimulates anxiety, particularly among blue-collar workers. People in Detroit, for example, complain about robots being used to build cars.

The behavior of others encourages anxiety. Even if you live 100 miles from the nearest prison, what happens if you hear: "We interrupt our regularly scheduled program to bring you this special report. Five men have escaped from. . . ." Immediately, you make sure all of your doors are locked.

Many single adults have family members or situations which bother-worry-frustrate-irritate-annoy. Or we have a friend or colleague whose behavior concerns us.

Assumptions and values are another source. If you were Amish, living in Pennsylvania Dutch country, you would never worry about your car starting when it was ten below zero. Why? The Amish do not drive cars. But the Amish can get most anxious if one of their horses strains a leg.

Simply, anxiety is a natural by-product of the type of world we live in.

UNDERSTANDING OUR ANXIETIES

Against our anxieties about the Russians, the Cubans, and the Chinese, to say nothing of Third World terrorists, consider Jesus' words from the Sermon on the Mount:

> Therefore, I tell you, do not worry about your life, what you will eat or drink; or about your body, what you will wear. Is not life more important than food, and the body more important than clothes? Look at the birds of the air; they do not sow or reap or store away in barns, and yet your Heavenly Father feeds them. Are you not *much more valuable* than they? Who of you by worrying can add a single hour to his life? (Matt. 6:25-27)

Prudent care is not forbidden by the Scripture. Rather it's anxious distraction which divides the mind in different directions. So rather than *deny* anxiety, Jesus offered guide lines for our response.

1. *Do not worry about your life* (Matt. 6:25). "Oh, but Jesus," we want to argue. Jesus' words echo like cannon fire: "Do not worry about your life!"—specifically what you will eat or drink. Isn't that a major Sunday morning agenda: deciding where to have brunch?

What about the anorexics who systematically starve themselves? Or those bulemics who are "stuffin' and puffin'"? I listened to one bulemic single (with two earned doctorates) confess to eating dog food because of her expensive obsession.

For single adults, THIN is IN!

2. *Do not worry about your body* (v. 25). Have you seen the calendars? The books? Our fixation is on "the body beautiful." How can Jesus say, "Don't worry about your body" to people who know how many calories are in a single carrot stick? Health clubs are the new singles' bars. People join to meet "someone" as well as to shape up.

Yet, fixation with the human body is still idolatry.

Jesus continued, "Or what you will wear." Nudity would solve some of our problems, but that is unacceptable for good reason. How many single adults whine, "What shall I wear?" or, "I don't have a thing to wear!" Yet, they carefully check the closet space before they move into an apartment.

Many single adults have to wear the latest fashions. They won't buy their jeans at Montgomery Ward either. They want "designer" clothes with little signatures on the label. I suspect that if some of those designers saw their signatures on some hips, they would rip off the labels.

It is so easy to buy clothes to make us look good or feel good or better about ourselves. The ads promise, "Look your best!" Though we spend a fortune, our pain and anxiety won't go away.

Rather Jesus says, "Look at the birds of the air" (v. 26). Frank Stagg observed that birds do not signify idleness but the absence of anxiety.[5] Have you ever seen an anxious bird? During Christmas I watched birds have a feast on scraps thrown into the snow. Big birds, small birds; mean, ugly birds. All chirping to their hearts' content.

Can you imagine a bird, flapping its wings frantically, moaning, *What am I gonna do if no one feeds me?* Hardly. The bird flies and glides in pursuit of food that he trusts will be there. If not in this neighborhood, then in the next.

Jesus also mentioned the lilies of the field as a model. "They do not labor or spin. Yet I tell you that not even Solomon in all his splendor was dressed like one of these" (Matt. 6:28-29). But that's too poetic to appeal to most consumers.

Jesus said, "Do not worry, saying, 'What shall we eat?' or 'What shall we drink?' or 'What shall we wear?'" Why? "For the pagans run after all these things" (vv. 31-32).

Anxiety is often caused and exaggerated by our lack of planning. Anxiety is caused or exaggerated by hasty, impulsive decisions. Two passages demonstrate this conclusion. First, "The steps of a good man" (or single adult) "are ordered by the Lord" (Ps. 37:23, KJV). God expects our decisions to be wise—to be the wise use of our resources. He expects us to rely on Him.

Secondly, Jesus used planning as an example of faithfulness. "Suppose one of you wants to build a tower" (or condo). "Will he not first sit down and estimate the cost to see if he has enough money to complete it? For if he lays the foundation and is not able to finish it, everyone who sees it will ridicule him, saying, 'This fellow began to build and was not able to finish'" (Luke 14:28-30). Jesus also warned about building "bigger barns" and thereby neglecting the real issues of life (Luke 12:18-20).

Anxiety is exaggerated by a lack of discipline. Single adults must learn "NO" power! Some of us are worrying about things today which we could have avoided *if* we had disciplined ourselves yesterday. Why did I have to go on a crash diet January 2nd? Because I had not been disciplined during the Christmas holidays. I could have enjoyed desserts in January if I had counted more calories during December.

The same is true spiritually and financially. Discipline is the gift we need.

Thirdly, Jesus said, "Do not worry about tomorrow" (Matt. 6:34). Even the pagans know that the tomorrow we dread may not come, or that tomorrow may be worse than we imagined! Sometimes, through a self-fulfilling prophecy, we create the tomorrow we feared.

There was a period in American history, roughly 1875 to 1900, when a major dispute erupted over Christians buying life insurance. Some saints thought it was definitely unspiritual since it denied trusting in God.

Sam Jones, the great Southern evangelist, deplored such logic. He urged people to first visit a "poor house" run by the county before they made a final decision. "That's where your wife and children will be getting their mail after you're gone!" This debate illustrates the cultural dimensions of our anxieties.

Frank Stagg summed it well, "*Whatever* you need to fulfill your calling, God will provide."[6] As the great hymnist noted, "All I have needed, Your hand has provided."[7] The crucial word is ***need*** rather than want. God will provide for our needs.

Anita Robertson concluded, "Just when you think He's all you have, you will find He's all you need!"[8] Once we have admitted our anxieties and have begun to understand them, we will still have them. Now we must discipline them.

DISCIPLINING OUR ANXIETIES

Do not be anxious over anything. Admittedly, that was easy for Paul to suggest in his day. But, review 2 Corinthians 11:23-28. What else could Paul have experienced? Paul had earned the right to say, "Don't be anxious."

Relax. Whatever happens, God is in control. And there is nothing that can happen that will overwhelm you.

Present your requests to God "in everything." By prayer, by petition, always with thanksgiving, make known your needs. As a result, "The peace of God, which transcends all understanding," (as well as our persistent "what if's") "will guard your hearts ***and your minds*** in Christ Jesus" (Phil. 4:7). In every crisis, Paul found peace. You too can find peace in the midst of your storms.

Choices dismantle anxiety. Psychiatrists Frank Minirth and Paul Meier offer some behavioral patterns and attitudes based on Scripture that will decrease anxiety:

- Determine to obey God.
- Pray.
- Realize that God can keep your mind safe.
- Meditate on positive thoughts.
- Focus on godly behavior.
- Divert attention from self to others.
- Work on being content.
- Realize that the grace of God is with you.[9]

Take a time out! I have a friend who lost his status with the airline industry just hours before he was entitled to permanent benefits. I asked him how he survived.

"I yelled, screamed, and pounded the floor for twenty-four hours. THEN I took a shower, ate a good meal, found the 'help-wanted ads' and went looking for a job." He set a limit on his anxiety.

Remember the angels. The angels are personally concerned about you. Henry Thiessen pointed out that angels are personal beings with spiritual tasks:

Angels have intelligence (1 Peter 1:12).
Angels have feelings (Luke 2:13).
Angels have wills (Jude 6).
Angels have responsibilities (Heb. 1:14).

Two of their responsibilities are giving encouragement (Acts 27:23-24) and caring for us (Luke 16:22; Jude 9; Matt. 18:10).[10] The psalmist insisted, "The angel of the Lord encamps around those who fear Him, and he delivers them" (Ps. 34:7). "*If* you make the Most High your dwelling—even the Lord, who is my refuge—then no harm will befall you, no disaster will come near your tent" (or condo). "For He will command His angels concerning you to guard you in *all* your ways; they will lift you up in their hands" (Ps. 91:9-12).

Seek first the kingdom! Kingdom citizenship realigns one's perspective on earthly and temporary things. The basic tenet is simple: "ASK and it will be given to you; SEEK and you will find; KNOCK and the door will be opened to you" (Matt. 7:7).

Seeking first the kingdom will not eliminate anxiety. But it will significantly reduce anxiety to manageable or ignorable and minimal levels. Thus, anxiety will not overwhelm you.

CONCLUSION

Anxiety is part of life's agenda. We can survive if our response is creative and resourceful and relies on God's care.

Let's review those questions from the beginning of this chapter.

- What are some consequences of my anxiety?
- Am I better off for having this anxiety?
- What nourishes my anxiety?
- How do others deal with this anxiety?
- How would Jesus deal with this anxiety?
- Why do I cling to this anxiety?
- How would I feel without this anxiety?

Ask one additional question. By reading this chapter, have I moved closer to abandoning or reducing my anxieties?

Anxieties may be initially forced upon us by circumstances. But if we become hospitable to our anxieties, it always requires decisions on our part.

I saw a plaque the other day with this simple calligraphy that captured my attention:

RICH is not how much you have
or where you are going
or even what you are
RICH is who you have beside you![11]

You *can* significantly reduce your anxieties as part of your agenda for adulthood.

COMING TO TERMS WITH GUILT

8

It's late at night. I am supposed to be on a diet. But I went to bed hungry and it's difficult for me to sleep when my stomach growls like a zoo! I know I could sleep better if I had a "little" snack.

So I raid the refrigerator. What a stockpile of caloric potentialities! Ah, there is one piece of apple pie left. It will probably spoil if left until morning. When I touch the plate, there is a cold shiver of anticipation. Now, realize that I am forgoing the two scoops of vanilla ice cream. Somewhere I read that calories consumed after midnight are less potent. Ah, ecstasy!

However, I soon conclude that the last few bites of crust need washing down.

Back to the refrigerator. A Pepsi would be wonderful, but that's too many calories. So how about a nice glass of cold milk?

The pie is gone and I drain the last of the milk from the glass. Sure was good!

One of the great things about being single is that when there is only one piece of pie left—it's all yours. You can reasonably be certain that the pie will still be there when you go to make sure the backdoor is locked at 1 A.M.

But let's examine the milk glass. Do you see the fine

residue—the milk coating on the glass? That's evidence of my diet transgression. Though I tried to drain every drop of milk from the glass, there is still enough residue to convince a grand jury.

The glass represents us; the milk represents guilt. A residue from some past experience remains to remind, to haunt, to harass. Guilt constantly spoils all of our tomorrows.

Many single adults ask, "What if tomorrow isn't better than yesterday?"

WHERE DO WE BEGIN?

Single adults need a model of someone who conquered guilt. If anyone had a right to feel guilty, it was the Apostle Paul. How did this man—this great single saint—deal with his memories as chief persecutor of the Christians?

As a brilliant rabbi who had studied with Gamaliel, Paul had been trained since youth to remember. Did he remember the screams of women as soldiers burst into their homes at night, carrying away their husbands—sons—fathers? Did he remember the groans as the stones killed the believers?

Did Paul remember the prayer of Stephen, the first martyr, "Lord Jesus, receive my spirit"? (Acts 7:59) Paul ran the coat-check according to Acts 7:58. He had to have heard Stephen's pain.

Luke described Saul's effort to destroy the early church. "Going from house to house, he dragged off men and women and put them in prison" (8:3). Paul went about his work with a religious enthusiasm breathing out "murderous threats against the Lord's disciples" (9:1). Until one day on the Damascus Road, the divine collision. In that intersection, Paul met Jesus.

Paul was stricken blind and had to be led away "by the hand" into Damascus (9:8). Meanwhile, in a vision, God had told Ananias to go to a house on Straight Street and see Paul. Now, Ananias was neither a hero nor a dummy. Probably a basic cautious analytical Jewish Christian. He responded, "*Lord,* I have heard many reports about this man and all the harm he has done to Your saints in Jerusalem. And he has come here with authority from the chief priests to arrest *all* who call on Your name" (9:13-14). Isn't it interesting how we inform the Lord of details that He already knows?

The Lord, however, insisted, "Go!" (v. 15) When Ananias met Paul, he gasped, "*Brother* Saul" (v. 17). Luke reports the power of God's guidance and enabling courage—Ananias affirmed the young convert. So Paul began to grow as a believer. When he preached he spoke so powerfully that the tables were turned. Paul now became the hunted, the persecuted. Paul fled to Jerusalem, but not into the open arms of the disciples. Hardly.

"He tried to join the disciples," Luke reported. "But they were all afraid of him, not believing that he really was a disciple" (9:26). That might have been the end of the story but for Barnabas' heroism. He personally escorted Paul to the apostles—sponsor-like.

If anyone knew guilt and remorse and was influenced by the potential of guilt, Paul did. Yet, he wrote, "One thing I do: forgetting what is behind and straining toward what is ahead, I press on toward the goal to win the prize for which God has called me heavenward in Christ Jesus" (Phil. 3:13-14).

Can you agree with Paul? Are you forgetting what is behind and straining toward what is ahead? Paul's statement initially sounds contradictory: "This *one* thing I do." Clearly, he lists *three* things: (1) forgetting; (2) straining; and (3) pressing on. Perhaps we should understand this as one system but with three stages.

STAGE ONE: FORGETTING WHAT IS BEHIND (THE PAST)

A good memory can be an asset and a good resource. But a good memory can also be a spiritual burden, particularly for those who are "savers" who keep everything, just in case. Peer into our closets, basements, garages, under the bed, under the kitchen sink. Oh, it may take us a while to retrieve it, but "it's here somewhere!"

As we are with items and objects, so we are with hurt and

memories. We store them. We keep them. But whatever we choose to store often "keeps" us tied to the past.

Paul had an incredible past. But from God's perspective he had an incredible future. Called to be an apostle to the Gentiles. Paul could have been emotionally sidetracked and hamstrung spiritually, if he had not come to terms with his past. He accomplished it through grace.

WHAT IS GRACE?

Grace is forgetting or letting go of the past. Paul Tournier explained in *Guilt and Grace,* "It is not guilt which is the obstacle to grace. On the contrary, it is the repression of guilt, self-justification, genuine self-righteousness and smugness which is the obstacle."[1]

Simply, denial keeps us from becoming friends with our pasts. Evangelicals have two strong traditions on the past. One system glorifies the past. During my childhood, a procession of ex-villains showed up at our church to "share" their wicked pasts. Ex-robbers, ex-junkies, whatevers. Just when you thought you had heard it all, along came another villain to tell his life story.

Like many kids, I grew up with a suspicion that in order to really serve God, I first needed to do something bad. The badder the better because that meant more glory for God and more "Hallelujah's!"

The second tradition is equally harmful. It's the Sister Hawkinses of the church with their long, long memories. They can recite indiscretions, bad judgments, embezzlements, adulteries, miscellaneous acts of fornication, rebelliousness, and mischief with incredible recall of particularly lurid details. They forget nothing that has happened to someone else.

One friend insists that he would much rather have the Lord catch him doing some things than other Christians. The Lord, he claims, would be easier and gentler.

Paul, however, could not ignore his past. There must have been some dear brothers and sisters in the early church who had a way of "digging up" the past whenever Paul dropped in for a visit. I have a friend who loves to attend church conferences. He'll spot some brother he's never met before and get a good look at his name badge. Then he will wait until the room is packed. From across the room, he will yell out, "Hey, Brother X. How did that situation ever turn out?"

Instantly, the brother's adrenalin is flowing. My friend says he has heard some of the strangest stories that way.

Surely, in one of those New Testament churches was a widow whose husband had been killed by Paul. Yet, Paul did not live in the past. Paul confessed, "I have been crucified with Christ and I no longer live, but Christ lives in me" (Gal. 2:20).

God is committed to forgiving and forgetting as part of the same process. If only singles could assume that same agenda. A bad memory may well be God's greatest characteristic. Can you sense the psalmist's excitement?

> The Lord is compassionate and gracious, slow to anger, abounding in love. He will not always accuse, nor will He harbor this anger forever; He does not treat us as our sins deserve or repay us according to our iniquities (Ps. 103:8-10).

The psalmist continues, "As far as the east is from the west, so far has He removed our transgressions from us" (v. 12). At what point does east become west?

I commented on this in my book *Forgiveness Is for Giving*. Suppose I board a plane and begin flying north from Kansas City. At a certain, exact point, I cross the North Pole and begin flying south. I can fly south for thousands of miles, but once I cross a certain line, I am flying north again. North and south are definite points.

However, it is possible to fly eastward forever because east is inseparable from the west. The psalmist's deliberate word choice should set us rejoicing!

"Oh, but you don't understand what I've done!" That's true, but the Lord does. He inserted no asterisks to say, "*Except* for the following classifications of sin."

Rather, "how much more, then, will the blood of Christ, who through the eternal Spirit offered Himself unblemished to God, cleanse our consciences from acts that lead to death, *so that we may serve the living God*" (Heb. 9:14).

We are freed from the past through Christ's death so that we may serve God without hesitation. So that we can be "confident and unashamed" (1 John 2:28).

But what about those moments when our mental videotapes overwhelm us? When we take on the role of prosecuting attorney hungry for a conviction? We do that well because we have access to all the evidence. John wrote that this is "how we set our hearts at rest in His presence *whenever* our hearts condemn us" (which suggests that the pattern of painful memory is normal). "For God is greater than our hearts, and He knows everything" (1 John 2:19-20).

God knows the worst about you and *still* loves you! Paul Ricoeur said, "What a wilderness it is when a Christian man has lost the sense of forgiveness while retaining his sense of sin!"[2] Or as Andrew Greeley observed in his novel, *Ascent into Hell*, "The worst sin in his life was to exempt himself from grace."[3]

That is why it is psychologically healthy and necessary to admit our failures. God already knows them. A small plaque hangs on my kitchen wall: *Our faults are more pardonable than the methods we think up to hide them!*[4]

Moreover, we are a community of the forgiven and the forgiving. Shakespeare noted, "The jury, passing on the prisoner's life, may in the sworn twelve have a thief or two, guiltier than him they try!"[5]

In the western territories in the late 1880s, when there weren't enough people to make up a jury, they often drafted prisoners. Reportedly they made tougher jurors.[6]

There are ministers and teachers who have built their reputations on a skill my dad calls "skinning 'em!" They specialize in getting people "down in the quick" over their pasts. But Jesus never does that.

Many of us delay our own healing. We keep our wounds festering because we pick at our scabs. The Lord whispers, "Leave the scabs alone. Trust Me with the scars."

The question is: What are you forgetting?

STAGE TWO: STRAINING TOWARD WHAT IS AHEAD (THE IMMEDIATE)

If you examined Paul's life, one reason he was *not* dwelling on his past was that he was too busy living in the present: teaching, preaching, making tents, instructing new believers. Paul could have wrapped his quilt of guilt around him and have been immobilized. Yet, Paul did not do that. He made a decision. He made a choice to strain.

Look at the steps in the straining.

STEP ONE: Abandon the ash heap. Sift around in your ashes. Some of you still smell like smoke. But it's time to stand up, to step up, and to abandon the ash heap. Maybe someone will offer you a hand; but you may have to lift yourself.

The God who heard Paul will hear you. God does not want you hampered by guilt, especially pseudo-guilt. He wants your tomorrows to be better than your yesterdays! John bubbled with enthusiasm as he wrote, "How great is the love the Father has lavished on us, that we should be called children of God!" (1 John 3:1) One hymnwriter noted:

O boundless love divine!
How shall this tongue of mine
To wond'ring mortals tell
  the matchless grace divine—
That I, a child of hell,
  should in His image shine!
The Comforter has come![7]

Have you allowed the ashes to overcome you? Have your senses been overcome by the constant whiffing of ashes? I recently discovered that the Army has to retire the dogs they have trained to sniff out drugs. After about eight years of sniffing, their sense of smell becomes "overwhelmed." The same is true with you.

What is God's agenda for you today? What is it that won't get done because you are sniffing ashes?

STAGE TWO: Don't look back! Lot's wife turned to a pillar of salt because she looked back (Gen. 19:26). There are a lot of single adults who are, in essence, salt pillars. There is a distinct human tendency to sabotage our own good by playing the games: *what if* or *if only*. Yet, Doug Manning warns, "Most 'if only's' are not really true. Even the ones that are true are beyond your control. There is nothing you can do to change them."[8]

You cannot relive yesterday. Let it be gone. The God who warned Lot, "Don't look back!" would say the same thing to you.

How do you spell relief from the past? Don't look back!

I have to deal with this constantly as a divorced person. Divorce is a stigma that I can never erase, even if I remarry. The label *Divorced* is an incredible yoke and burden. It breaks the spirits, destroys the dreams, suffocates the creativity of so many. Yet, a few decide, like oxen, to become familiar with the yoke of the stigma and get on with life.

But, there are some people who have problems with my past. It's not past history to them. It's as fresh as yesterday.

Some think that I have "gotten away" with divorce. They proof-text, "You'll reap what you sow—God will not be mocked" (see Gal. 6:7). While that may be true, there is the balancing reality of Psalm 103:10: "He does not treat us as our sins deserve!"

Unfortunately, some single adults have created a God who is like them. Who nurses grudges and keeps score. Who stores up anger. Who settles scores mafioso style. God the Executioner. Paul Tournier spoke on this point.

> The notion that everything has to be paid for is very deep-seated and active within us, as universal as it is unshakable by logical argument. The people who most ardently long for grace have the greatest difficulty in accepting it.[9]

How sad! These people wait for the rug to be yanked out from under them by a vengeance-seeking God. But the Bible "offers them assurance that God removes the guilt *of anyone* who suffers from it, and that by His severity He arouses guilt so as to lead them in their turn to the same experience of grace."[10]

Tournier says we need to understand God's aim. His

justice "aims, not to suppress the arrogant sinner but to arouse his sense of guilt, so as to humble him, thereby opening for him, the way to grace."[12]

For a long time we have been taught that guilt is bad. Perhaps, we thought it to be like pain. Something to be avoided. But guilt, like pain, is a trend indicator that something is wrong. It's a warning signal. Guilt is a valuable human feeling, essential to the survival of the species.

Some psychiatrists suggest that the growing violence in our society is because we have anesthetized ourselves against guilt.

STEP THREE: Don't overlook the blue lights. Many single adults confuse guilt with guilty fear. Suppose you're going 65 m.p.h. on an interstate highway and pass a parked police car. The fear of being caught, ticketed, and fined (especially the latter) is a primary response. But you do not have an internalized sense of having done something wrong.

You will possibly inform the officer if he pulls you over, "There were plenty of other people going faster than me." Or, you may threaten not to contribute to the next fund-raiser sponsored by the Fraternal Order of Police.

However, your guilty fear evaporates when the policeman pulls over a trucker instead of you.

You are still guilty, aren't you? You broke the speed limit. But you were not "caught."

Some single adults become so emotionally and spiritually crippled that they cannot deal with their guilt. They become obsessed with their failures or sins. Some had unrealistic goals and expectations; they set out to fail. Some only feel good when they feel bad. A few even become proud of their guilt because it appears to be a thermometer of their spirituality.

That's why Paul put into context the teaching on eating of meat that had been offered to idols. All of us have different thresholds of temptation. We must bear with the weaker brother or sister (1 Cor. 8:1-13).

Are you straining toward what is ahead? Or at some gnat in your past? Can you do anything about it? If so, do it! But if not, forget it!

STAGE THREE: PRESSING ON TOWARD THE GOAL (THE FUTURE)

Paul never lost sight of his goal. A lot of people could have been in the last Olympics, but few people made the team because few were willing to become obsessed with winning the gold. One doesn't merely slip into Nikes and sweatpants to make the team. An Olympic athlete focuses on one thing: the best. Winning comes at the end of a long trail.

What was Paul's goal? "To win the prize for which God has called me" (Phil. 3:14). "To take hold of that for which Christ Jesus took hold of me" (v. 12). The prize was eternal life. In the homestretch of his race, Paul did not intend to allow any distractions. He could see the finish line in his mind.

If you are going to reach your goal, I would suggest some basic principles, if tomorrow is to be better than yesterday.

1. *Forgiveness is a decision for a better tomorrow.* Remember the prodigal son's words in the hog pen? "*I will arise* and go to my father" (Luke 15:18, KJV). He made a decision to abandon his past.

Paul declared, "There is now *no* condemnation for those who are in Christ Jesus" (Rom. 8:1). That is like money in the bank in a checking account. It's valueless until you write a check against that balance.

Some singles are very forgiving and forgetting of others. Dare to be as generous with yourself. Forgiveness is not a feeling or emotion. It is always a decision. Better tomorrows result from today's decisions.

2. *Forgiveness is a pilgrimage to a better tomorrow.* Forgiveness is a journey, not a destination. Some wounds take time to heal. God wants us to take the first step. People occasionally leaf through one of my books and say, "This took a lot of work." Yeah, but it was one word at a time, a page at a time. I tell those who want to write a book and don't know where to begin: Start with the *first* word of the *first* sentence of the *first* paragraph of the *first* chapter of the *first* book.

Forgiveness is a pilgrimage. A commitment to staying on

the main road, not wandering down the side streets, until forgiveness becomes a reality.

3. *Forgiveness is a reality.* Forgiveness is not some abstract ideal but is a reality in which we can participate. Forgiveness is one of the two godlike powers given to mankind. I think this is why people spend millions on therapists, psychologists, and counselors. Some of them are so close to forgiveness, but somehow they miss it and spoil another tomorrow.

4. *Forgiveness paves the way for new dreams.* Ever stuff leftovers into the refrigerator? The next night, however, a friend invites you to eat with him. You forget the leftovers. Two weeks later, an awful smell permeates your kitchen. As you investigate the source of the smell, you find a plastic container. You peel back the lid to find green, moldy, foul-smelling chili.

Well, some of us have our spirits packed full of plastic containers, packed with the wrongs and woes that have befallen us. We need a cleaning! Not to make room for new containers of fresh guilt—but to give us freedom to breathe.

CONCLUSION

Tomorrow can be better than yesterday! Whether your yesterday was a divorce, a broken engagement, a firing, a premarital pregnancy, or whatever—tomorrow can be better!

Almost all of the Bible's great people of faith knew failure. Many earned notoriety for their failures as well as for their achievements. Yet, they gained prominence through God's grace. Paul was able to say, "My dear brothers, stand firm. Let *nothing* move you" (1 Cor. 15:58). *Nothing* includes the past.

We all have a "worst thing that could happen" to us scenario recorded in our minds. What would I do if X found out about ________________? Christ invites us to surrender *all* of our yesterdays and our fears to Him.

Let me offer a paraphrase of Paul's great declaration in Romans: "For I am convinced that neither death nor life, neither angels nor demons, *neither the past, the present, nor the future,* nor any powers, neither height nor depth, nor anything else in all creation, will be able to separate us from the love of God that is in Christ Jesus our Lord" (8:38-39).

Paul changed history because he forgot; he strained; and he pressed on. He won the prize and by following his example we too may gain that prize.

Some single adults cling tightly to the past. But the past is like a piece of glass. The tighter I squeeze, the more deeply the glass cuts.

Jesus wants us to open our hands and let Him have the glass. From the broken pieces of our lives, He makes stained-glass windows.

Tomorrow can be better than yesterday *if* you come to terms with your guilt.

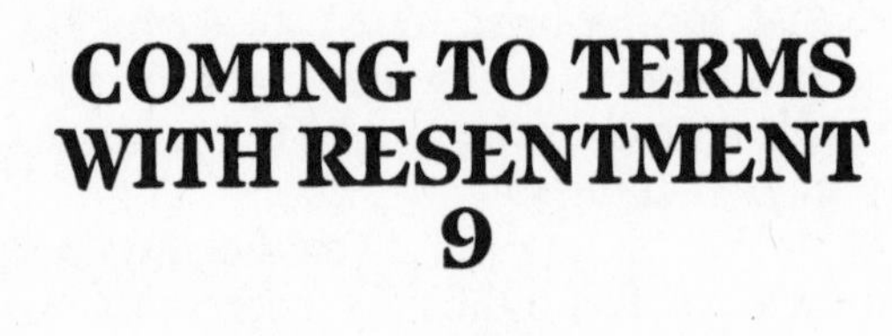

COMING TO TERMS WITH RESENTMENT
9

With all the current fascination with professional wrestling, I have wished that we could create wrestling matches for people who have differences. Grudges are the direct by-product of resentment. Webster defines *resentment* as "to show or feel displeasure and indignation at some (act, remark) or toward a person from a sense of being injured or offended."

Have you ever wondered why some talented, skilled, beautiful people can't get their acts together? Kenneth Gangel in *Leadership for Christian Education* warned of four barriers to healthy self-esteem. Gangel suggested grudges interact with defensiveness, insecurity, and jealousy to harm the witness, influence, and happiness of believers.[1]

The writer of Hebrews warned, "*Make every effort* to live in peace with all men and to be holy. . . . See to it that . . . no bitter root grows up to cause trouble and to defile many" (Heb. 12:14-15).

ADMITTING RESENTMENT

You seldom get help for a problem that you deny. There has to be a moment when you "own up" to your needs—however unpleasant. That's why resentment is a spiritual battleground for many single adults. It's the tug-of-war between the whispers:

"You shouldn't feel this way!"
versus
"You have a right to feel this way!"

Some single adults are better than others at denying their resentment. They sink their hurts deeply into the subconscious. Denial, however, leads to festering. Like a malignant tumor, it feeds on healthy cells. No wonder Paul was so concerned.

In 2 Samuel 15 we find David fleeing his son, Absalom, who had revolted. Can you sense his humiliation in this passage? "David continued up the Mount of Olives, weeping as he went; his head was covered and he was barefoot. And all the people with him covered their heads too and were weeping as they went up" (15:30).

Suddenly, on the horizon, Shimei appeared. The last man who had "appeared" had brought bread, raisins, figs, and wine. But Shimei was not from Welcome Wagon. He did three things to David: (1) he cursed; (2) he pelted; and (3) he accused. "Get out, get out, you man of blood, you scoundrel!" Shimei shouted at David (16:7). Pretty tough words to hurl at the king.

David didn't chant back, "Sticks and stones may break my bones." David knew that words could hurt. Shimei's epithets only added to his anguish.

When I was growing up, the vacant lot next door was the site of many dirtclod battles. Dirtclods generally hurt your pride more than your skin. But occasionally, when the battle turned too aggressive, the words also zinged back and forth. Sometimes I wanted to give my adversary a dirtclod sandwich.

Often, the taunts and boasts *after* the fight broke up were much worse than the fight had been. I remember glaring at an opponent, daring him to say one more word. Then came the decision: would I walk away or start round two?

Abishai, son of Zeruiah, was a neighborhood bully, itching for a fight—even if he had to create one. Abishai snarled, "Why should this dead dog curse my lord the king? Let me go over and cut off his head!" (16:9)

Dead dog was hardly a compliment. Fred Young explained that in this time period, a dog was "a scavenger and usually diseased—a despised, shameless, and miserable creature."[2] Moreover, cursing the king was a capital offense. Abishai was a good "law and order" man.

David, however, rebuked Abishai rather than Shimei. That must have stung Abishai's pride. David believed that he was being cursed at God's direction (v. 12), so why should he protest?

David had no problem with his hearing. Though the verbal abuse compounded his mental anguish, he made a decision. "David and his men continued along the road" (v. 13). Sometimes, one simply has to continue along the road until things improve. Shimei probably became all the more boisterous, more outrageous, more vicious since he now knew nothing would be done to him. As a result, "the king and all the people with him arrived at their destination exhausted" (v. 14). They were both physically and emotionally exhausted and that breeds resentment.

Next we look at 2 Samuel 19, after Absalom's death and the quelling of the revolt. The political crisis had been dramatically reversed. David was now firmly in control. As a result, Shimei was in big trouble. Since Absalom had been defeated, Shimei had to make amends to David. Shimei "hurried down with the men of Judah to meet King David" (2 Sam. 19:16). Crossing the Jordan, Shimei "fell prostrate before the king" and pleaded, "Do not hold me guilty; do not remember my offense; and put it out of your mind" (see vv. 18-19).

What a big request from such a guilty man! Still, Shimei did not clearly own up to his guilt. Nor did he say, "I'm sorry." Shimei skirted the issue. No doubt he *was* sorry that Absalom had died. Shimei exhibited a classic case of guilty fear: *David's going to kill me!*

Watch how he polished the apple. "Today I have come here as the first of the whole house of Joseph to come down and meet my lord the king" (v. 20). What a dramatic change of attitude! No doubt some of his catchy phrases still echoed in David's memory.

Again, Abishai, son of Zeruiah, happened to be present. "Shouldn't Shimei be put to death for this?" he snapped. "He cursed the Lord's anointed!" (v. 21)

You can always count on someone to remember "chapter and verse." Abishai was an ancient Frank Burns (from the MASH unit), always quoting Army regulations. Such men have two key words in their vocabularies: *should* and *shouldn't*.

Tragically, Christian "hit men" today mimic Abishai. They know the *shouldn'ts* and volunteer to be executioners. Unfortunately, in the army of the Lord, there seems to be no shortage of volunteers for positions on the *next* firing squad. Some will even supply their own ammunition.

Today, a lawyer might try to argue that Shimei was insane or insist on a technicality. "Certainly, my client did curse the Lord's anointed—*but only* because he did not know, at the particular moment in question, that David was *still* the Lord's anointed." And a jury might buy that defense.

David, however, responded as he did in the earlier episode: "What do you and I have in common?" (v. 22)

Shimei waited for judgment. He expected the swoosh of the sword that would dispatch him forthwith to Sheol's darkness. You've seen that technique in movies. The executioner plays with the victim by placing the gun against the man's head and clicking the trigger—only the gun isn't loaded. That's incredible psychological pain!

After what seemed an eternity, the king assured Shimei, "You shall not die" (v. 23). Instant relief. David promised not to execute him. You can almost sense the disappointment on Abishai's face and the relief on Shimei's.

Years passed until "the time drew near for David to die" (1 Kings 2:1). He counseled Solomon, "I am about to go the way of all the earth. So be strong, show yourself a man, and observe what the Lord your God requires" (2:2-3). Three good pieces of advice. If only David had stopped there.

In what follows, David sounded more like a mafioso godfather than the psalmist. If only this great leader—who had experienced so much grace—had bestowed grace in dying. Instead David ordered:

> And remember, you have with you Shimei son of Gera, the Benjamite from Bahurim, who called down bitter curses on me the day I went to Mahanaim. . . . But now, do not consider him innocent. You are a man of wisdom; you will know what to do to him. Bring his gray head down to the grave in blood (2:8-9).

This was David's great blemish; far greater, in my judgment, than his sin with Bathsheba. Shimei's insults had festered for years in David's soul and contaminated his memory and his mercy.

Solomon accepted David's burden. This burden could have gone to the grave with David. But vengeance became a top priority item on the new king's agenda. Solomon ordered Shimei into exile. "Do not go anywhere else. The day you leave and cross the Kidron Valley, you can be sure you will die; your blood will be on your own head" (2:36-37).

Shimei agreed. What other choice did he have?

So "Shimei stayed in Jerusalem for a long time" (v. 38). No vacations; no family reunions; no out-of-town conventions. Three boring years until two of Shimei's slaves ran away. Look at the wording, "Shimei was told, 'Your slaves are in Gath'" (v. 39). Do you catch the whiff of intrigue? A setup? Look at verse 41, "When Solomon was told. . . ."

It's there, isn't it? Someone's out to get Shimei. Perhaps Shimei went into Solomon's presence assuming that the king had not heard of his little excursion down to Gath to search for the slaves (v. 40). But Solomon knew. Why? "He had been told."

Shimei detected Solomon's undertone when he said, "You know in your heart all the wrong you did to my father David" (v. 44). Shimei could have protested, "That's old business." But Shimei quickly concluded the consequences. Quickly, Benaiah, son of Jehoiada "went out and struck Shimei down and killed him" (v. 46). Abishai must have been disappointed again.

Beware of angering those with long memories and long swords. Beware of making room for resentment. If David—a "man after God's own heart"—got tangled up in resentment, so can you.

UNDERSTANDING RESENTMENT

What are some characteristics of resentment?

1. *Resentment is a reasonable temptation.* You have been offended, insulted, or hurt. At some point you concluded, *I have a right to feel the way I do about this.* You may have added, *You'd feel the same way if it had happened to you!*

Unfair, unjust things happen to all of us. Unfortunately, some single adults attract more than their fair share. The enemy will attempt to convince you that you have a right to resent so-and-so. Particularly when there are long-term consequences.

I admire MADD, Mothers Against Drunk Drivers. Yet I would like to remind them that their anger and resentment cannot bring back their loved ones.

From the world's perspective, resentment is reasonable.

2. *Resentment is really anger rehashed.* As I jogged one hot August day in San Diego, a woman made a few unflattering comments about my sweating body. Boy, was I annoyed!

About a half-mile later, I thought of the greatest one-liner and turned back to deliver it. Quickly, I realized that would have meant an extra mile on my run and I was already exhausted. So I ran home. That night I rehearsed my put-down over and over.

The next morning, I was ready. As I neared her apartment complex, the insult was poised, ready for launching. But she wasn't there! Nor the next day, nor the next. A year passed. I was still "cued-up," but I never saw her again.

It is always dangerous to replay insults in our minds. Those "I should have saids" or "I should have dones" are lethal.

Joseph Kennedy coached his sons, "Don't get mad—get even!" But whenever I rekindle, reexamine, or reignite the insults, I haven't resolved the problem. Hindsight may give a perspective and offer a clever retort, but plotting rarely solves the problem.

3. *Be cautious in accepting another's resentment.* Heirlooms and trinkets are passed down from generation to generation; some are of such value that they cannot be appraised. But some heirlooms convey pain. We cannot choose the family into which we are born. But we *can* decide which of our family's prejudices, biases, and stored resentments we will assume.

The ultimate tragedy of Solomon was to accept his father's emotional agenda. What David had not been able to accomplish, Solomon did. His construction of the temple was noble, but his actions with Shimei were dastardly!

4. *Resentment contaminates.* Have you ever seen an oil slick or spill? The oil contaminates everything it touches. It may be a beautiful picture-postcard beach that is a pleasant memory in the minds of thousands. But if an oil slick touches it, the beach is devastated, perhaps destroyed.

Resentment cannot be easily contained or "mopped up." It infects! It contaminates! It destroys! From the world's perspective, you may well have a right to your resentments, but with the rights come the consequences.

There is a direct correlation between what you choose to hate or resent and what will kill you. Resentment, like anger, eventually affects the body as well as the spirit. Resentment destroys relationships, friendships, partnerships, even trust between colleagues. If camouflaged, resentment becomes even more destructive.

Those are four of the characteristics of resentment. Who are the recipients of your resentment?

Family?
Mate?
Parents?
Colleagues?
Children?
Fellow workers?
Employer?
Former mate?
Neighbors?
Minority groups?

Perhaps you resent whole groups of people. Look at the difficulty facing many Haitians because some have been linked to AIDS. Some people resent blacks or Mexicans. The young resent the old; the old resent the young. Working people resent the unemployed; the unemployed resent employed people. The taxpayer resents the government bureaucrat; the bureaucrat resents the tax-griper. Management resents union; union resents management.

Some Detroit autoworkers resent certain automobiles. Try parking your Datsun or Toyota in their neighborhood.

Some singles resent strangers or newcomers. Members of one single adult group complained that they were growing too rapidly. "It was much better when it was just us," their leader said, wondering if I could help them stop growing. However, Scripture urges hospitality: "Do not forget to entertain strangers, for by so doing some people have entertained angels without knowing it" (Heb. 13:2).

Some single adults even resent God. They wonder, *Why does God allow this to happen to me?* Or, *If God loves me so much, how come He hasn't brought a man or woman into my life?* Such questions made Harold Kushner's *When Bad Things Happen to Good People* an overnight bestseller.

The possibilities for resentment are limitless. So far, we have considered the characteristics of resentment and the recipients of resentment. Now let's look at motivations. The same experience can happen to two people, both of whom will be hurt. However, ten years later one vividly remembers every detail. The other barely remembers. Why?

WHAT MOTIVATES RESENTMENT?

1. *Unresolved anger.* Some people have been taught that it is wrong to be angry. Some have heard it put more strongly: It's a sin!

Consider Paul. He instructed the Ephesians, "In your anger do not sin. Do not let the sun go down while you are still angry, and do not give the devil a foothold" (Eph. 4:26-27).

A good emotional outburst or explosion can be therapeutic. Watch two children scrapping. To hear them, you'd think they were lifetime enemies. Thirty minutes later, it's "milk-and-cookies" time. Children do not hold grudges; they have to be taught to hold grudges.

Eliminate your resentment. That's practical advice.

2. *Unsolved dilemmas.* Something bothers us, especially if it happened in a confusing or vulnerable moment. Naturally, we try to dissect it to make sense. But some things, some events will NEVER make sense this side of eternity. So your *Why did this happen to ME?* is wasted. A college president once gave me a wise piece of advice: "It's not so much what happens to you, but how you *choose* to respond."

3. *Fear of recurrence.* Sometimes, resentment is fueled by the fear that the experience will occur again. That we will be just as helpless, just as vulnerable the second time.

Abraham experienced that fear when he went down to Egypt. Afraid that the Egyptians would kill him because of Sarah's beauty, he urged her, "Say you are my sister, so that I will be treated well for your sake and my life will be spared because of you" (Gen. 12:13).

Sure enough, the Pharaoh confiscated Sarah for his harem and the Lord had to inflict a few serious diseases on his household. Sarah got expelled from the harem and Abraham got a stern lecture on honesty (vv. 15-20).

Lesson learned, right? Wrong! In Gerar, Abimelech confiscated Sarah for his harem (20:3). Again, Abraham fudged, "She is my sister" (v. 3). Again, the Lord threatened to inflict a serious consequence (death) on a passionate king (vv. 3-7). Again, another expulsion and honesty lecture (vv. 8-17).

Fear does strange things to people, even patriarchs. The problem begins in childhood when our parents punished us and demanded that we promise that the behavior would not be repeated. But it was. Perhaps, the second time we were punished more severely. That same fear taunts many today.

4. *Helplessness.* "I feel so helpless!" we exclaim. We live in a world where power is the name of the game. "Who you know" is a reality. Sometimes we lose, not fairly or squarely, but because of manipulation. If the rules had been followed, we would have won. But we lost and we resent that.

5. *Refusal to accept responsibility. He did it!* or *It's all his fault!* are common clichés. But things are seldom *all* anyone's fault. We want someone to blame; we anxiously twist or

interpret facts to support *our* point of view. It began in the Garden with Adam's, "The woman You put here with me—she gave me some fruit from the tree, and I ate it" (Gen. 3:12). Excuses will continue until the sunset of man's existence. But they rarely contribute to understanding.

6. *Refusal to accept an outcome or result.* In 1960, John Kennedy was elected President by a narrow margin. The election may have been decided in Chicago where suspicious things happened at the polls (such as dead people voting). Despite evidence of voter fraud, Richard Nixon conceded the election because he didn't want the presidency to be paralyzed.

From this vantage point, I wonder about Nixon's psychological feelings toward Kennedy in those years. Did resentment overwhelm him? Did it lead to a fixation on the Oval Office that ultimately led to Nixon's betrayal of the confidence of the American people?

Sometimes you've got to look up at the scoreboard and cry; then head for the locker room. Whether you won or lost, you need a shower. Life goes on. There is life after the game.

It takes more than admitting or understanding resentment to limit its consequences. David made choices. He could have totally forgiven Shimei. What an example that would have been for Solomon as well as for us. But David did not discipline his gnawing resentment.

As he lay dying—perhaps, all along—David replayed old videotapes. That choice stirred up the flames of smoldering resentment and led ultimately to Shimei's death.

DISCIPLINING RESENTMENT

I've got to be me! is the theme of many single adults. That explanation means that *you* should excuse their behavior or attitudes. After all, they are just being themselves.

Some people have learned to discipline their resentment. Here are some guidelines that they have learned.

1. *Refuse to play the old videotapes.* When you are feeling "blue," it's tempting to put on a stack of old memories and grieve. Some folks really get into the painful but "precious"

memories. One widower resents *all* doctors because his wife died under poor medical care. He carries around a picture of her in her casket. He still whips the picture out of his wallet and laments his sad story—ten years later!

Memories are a choice. Sometimes, you must simply refuse to watch the reruns of yesterday's hurts.

2. *Refuse to repeat the situation.* By the time you have repeated the incident—emphasizing the *Woe is me* aspect and have gained the listener's sympathy—reality may be thin. A chorus of "My! My! My's!" encourages you to embellish, to emphasize certain points while overlooking others. You may convince yourself that the incident was worse than you actually experienced.

3. *Relinquish innocence.* Honestly ask, *What did I do to contribute to the problem?* Try to see the other person's point of view.

4. *Time heals all wounds, but a healthy dose of effort on our part helps.* Some hurts will not disappear overnight so we must "befriend" the pain. Time has a way of healing when we do not pick at the scabs.

5. *Rid yourself of all claim checks to justice.* Look at some common expressions of resentment:

"I'll get even with you if it's the last thing I ever do."

"I'll get you, one way or the other."

"Don't think I'm going to forget this."

"You'll get yours!"

Sometimes, we want to wait around long enough to enjoy the prophetic fulfillment of our resentment (or even assist the fulfillment). But what about God's statement, "It is mine to avenge; I will repay"? (Heb. 10:30)

Resentment begins with the INCIDENT (what happened), then proceeds to the EMBELLISHMENT (what you say or think happened). At this point, you face a CROSSROADS. If you allow the event to expand, you create a malignancy. Or you can choose to dismantle your resentment.

After that the range of consequences is endless. Still, at any stage, the decision is yours: You *choose* to surrender your claim checks or *choose* to buy even more lottery tickets.

In elementary school, one of my favorite stories was about a little boy who found a bear cub in the woods. The cub was cute and furry and the boy needed a friend. He took the cub home and hid him in the smokehouse.

The boy took good care of the cub and fed him and fed him and fed him. Pretty soon the cub grew to become a bear—unpredictable and unmanageable. That same process works with humans.

Some of you have carried home resentments, thinking that you could control them. You've fed them. Now those resentments, like the bear, are unmanageable.

One of my favorite Bible verses is this: "Like water spilled on the ground, which cannot be recovered, so we must die. But God does not take away life; instead, He devises ways so that a banished person may not remain estranged from Him" (2 Sam. 14:14).

God devises ways. David could have devised a way to have diffused the painful, haunting memories of Shimei's accusations. You, through the power of God in you, can terminate your resentments. Don't renew the lease. Devise ways to restore and renew relationships and rebuild trust.

What do you think about when you see the word *Irish?* The color green? Leprechauns? Shamrocks? St. Patrick's Day?

Patrick lived between 400 and 490 A.D. He was captured by pirates and taken to North Ireland and sold into slavery as a shepherd. Day after day, Patrick sat in solitude, longing for his home and family. More than once he probably mumbled, "If I ever get a chance to escape. . . ." or "If I ever get my hands on those pirates. . . ."

Yet Patrick discovered God. He later explained:

> In a strange land, the Lord opened the blind eyes of my unbelief, so that I thought, though at a late hour, of my sins, and turned with my whole heart to the Lord. He looked down upon my low estate, my ignorance, my youth. He cared for me before I knew Him, and before I could distinguish good from evil. He protected and comforted me, as a father his son.[3]

After six years of slavery, Patrick escaped! He went home to a joyous reunion with his family. Ten years passed. Again, he was captured; again, he escaped. His resentment multiplied.

What horrid memories of slavery he had. Then in a dream he heard voices pleading in an Irish dialect, "We beseech thee, child of God, come and walk among us, again."

What? Return to the land of slavery? Never! But Patrick recognized the voice of God as well. Patrick returned to Ireland and gathered the peasants around him in the open fields to preach to them. He started hundreds of churches and baptized 100,000 converts. Patrick lived to be not an embittered man, but one of the greatest missionaries of all time.[4]

Why? Because through the grace of God he *overcame* his tragedy and the further tragedy of resentment.

Resentment has long-lasting consequences. It destroys your ability to trust others, your ability to be self-critical, and your deep sense of self-assurance and confidence. Is dealing with resentment on your agenda?

QUESTIONS

Following are some questions that you should ask if you want to avoid David's footsteps.

1. What are some potential consequences of this resentment?
2. Am I better off for having this resentment?
3. How or when did this resentment begin? (You're in big trouble if you cannot remember.)
4. How would others deal with this resentment?
5. What keeps me from abandoning this resentment?

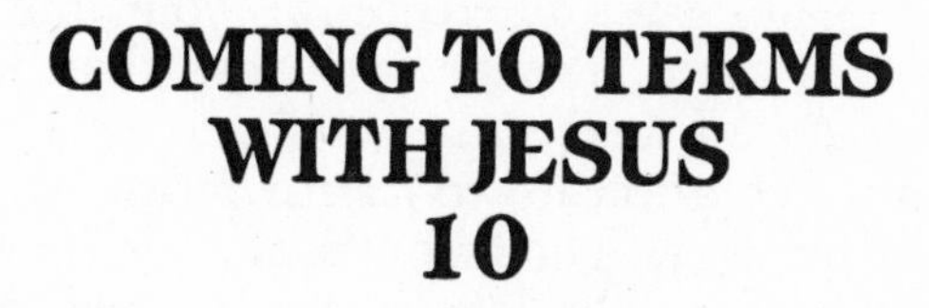

COMING TO TERMS WITH JESUS
10

My dad likes to listen to radio preachers, especially those who are practitioners of the art of "skinnin' 'em" or getting people "down into the quick." One day, while riding in the car with him, we were listening to one firebrand. While I am all for "honoring father and mother," I had had my fill of theological inaccuracy, proof-texting, and exaggeration—to say nothing of weird breathing patterns.

"Dad, would you mind if I turned that mess off?"

"Wasn't for that 'mess' you wouldn't be in this world," he replied.

"Huh?"

"Just what I said. Wasn't for them, you wouldn't be here!"

"Would you mind explaining that?" I asked.

"That evangelist held a revival in our church in 1946."

"Dad, I wasn't born until 1947."

"And one night he preached against birth control. Said every good Christian couple ought to have another child to replace the men that had been killed in World War II. So, your mom and I, being patriotic and all that—well, we had you."

My outburst of laughter was not well received. "Laugh all you want, sonny boy. But it's true!"

"Noooo!" I protested.

"How many days difference in your birthday and Ronnie's?" Dad asked. Ronnie is a close church friend.

"Three days," I answered.

Then my dad proceeded to further prove his point with other "close" birthdays. Nine months after that revival, there had been proof of the obedience of the evangelist's listeners. So I know why I was born. My mom and dad believed in doing what the preacher said.

Why were you born? For what great spiritual reason were you given to this world? Bruce Larson asked, "What did God dream for you the first time He thought of you?"[1]

Anita Robertson did a remarkable calligraphy on that thought.

WHEN GOD WANTS SOMETHING GREAT
DONE IN THIS WORLD

He doesn't dispatch a legion of avenging angels;
Neither does He call forth a whirlwind nor ignite the fuse of volcanic fireworks;
No commandeering of troops into battle nor discharging zealous crusaders to holy causes;
He does not orchestrate the burst and boom of thunder nor display His fiery arrows' majesty across the sky to bring His purpose to pass.
When God wants something great done in this world . . .
He sends a baby and then . . . He waits.[2]

We like Christmas and the Christmas stories about the birth of Jesus. Though Matthew and Luke tell us about the birth, John focuses instead on the *why* of the birth.

If I asked you, "Why was Jesus born?" you would no doubt respond, "To save us." Ah, but what about the step beyond Calvary? "Saved to what?"

Jesus said, "I have come that they may have life, and have it to the full" (John 10:10). Some translations read, "abundantly." That word is hard to say without enthusiasm. Try mumbling abundantly. Jesus declared, "I am come that single adults might have life and have it more abundantly!"

How does Christ's coming, living, and dying affect you? How does His resurrection? What did Christ accomplish through His life? Should there be any difference between Christian single adults and Hindu or Buddhist singles?

Jesus delivered and delivers us from four inadequate systems of thinking so that we can live abundant lives. Clearly, thinking precedes living, after all, "as [a single] thinketh, in his heart, so is he" (Prov. 23:7, KJV). Many leaders have tried to alter single adult lifestyles and specific behaviors. Such efforts are futile until we change the thinking (or lack of thinking) that motivates the behaviors.

JESUS FREES SINGLES FROM ARK THINKING

If I had to select a word that summarizes the Old Testament view of an individual, it would be *family*—a paradox since an individual is not a family. That's why the genealogies and long lists of names appear and reappear throughout the Old Testament.

The Jews had no strong concept of eternal life. They had *sheol,* a feared place. They did not have a heaven to long for. Their concept of immortality was based on the continuation of the seed, generation after generation. Thus, thousands of years after Abraham, we still talk about "the sons of Abraham."

You possibly have an aunt who occasionally quotes, "It is not good for the man to be alone"—which leads her to ask, "Why aren't you married?" Some aunts use a tone of voice, a slight vocal inference to suggest something that is not in the Hebrew: That *everyone* ought to get married!

This is one of the rallying points of some who have a problem with singlehood. One conservative noted:

> The single man in general is disposed to criminality, drugs and violence. He is irresponsible about his debts, alcoholic, accident prone, and venereally diseased. Unless he can marry, he is often destined to a Hobbsean life—solitary, poor, nasty, brutish and short.[3]

I contrast such a view with my friend in an Indiana monastery. He's hardly solitary, nasty, or brutish. He once talked to me about the goals of a man: to father a son, to plant a tree, and to write a book. I responded, "I planted my tree (it died), I've written my books, but I have no son." In essence he was asking, "What good are these blessings when I have no son?"

This good monk helped me see the number of spiritual sons I have influenced. When his singleness gets to him, he visits his brother who has eight children. "After a few days," he laughed, "I am ready for the monastery again."

But he paused. "You Protestants so misunderstand our 'prayers for the dead.' What was your great-great-grandfather's name?"

When I hesitated, he prodded, "Any of them—you had eight."

I couldn't name one.

"Ah," he smiled. "Later today I will pray for the dead. Not to get them out of hell, but to *remember* them. To specifically call them by name. Today, some Franciscan monk, who didn't have children, who has been dead for 300 years will be remembered specifically by name. And 300 years from my death, if the Lord tarries, a Franciscan will call my name too."

Before Christ's birth one of the worst things that could happen was to be either a eunuch (for a male) or to be barren (for a woman). Check the emotional anguish Hannah suffered during her barrenness (see 1 Sam. 1–2). Isaiah countered, "Let not any eunuch complain, 'I am only a dry tree,'" which translated means, *I am a worthless member of society.*

> For this is what the Lord says: To the eunuchs [single adults] who keep My Sabbaths, who choose what pleases Me and hold fast to My covenant—to them I will give within My temple and its walls a memorial and a name better than sons and daughters; I will give them an everlasting name that will not be cut off (Isa. 56:4–5).

Jesus reminds us that marriage is a temporary thing, of

this earth. The Sadducees came to Jesus with a question about a woman who had serially married seven brothers. They asked, "Whose wife will she be?"

Jesus, aware of the thoughts behind the question, answered, "At the resurrection people will neither marry nor be given in marriage; they will be like the angels in heaven" (Matt. 22:30).

The psalmist observed, "A righteous man" (married or single) "will be remembered forever" (Ps. 112:6).

I believe the New Testament is soft on the nuclear family. Instead the writers mentioned "the household of faith," which isn't limited to mama-papa and two offspring. Moreover, the New Testament question is not *Were you married or single?* but rather *Are you His?*

No one in his right mind would have said to Corrie ten Boom, "Oh, you poor half-person. You never had a family of your own! How unfulfilled you must have been!"

Why? Because Corrie was a kingdom-seeker. She didn't sit around waiting for Prince Charming to appear. Rather than being self-seeking or mate-seeking, Corrie changed the world by seeking first His kingdom.

But what if I die without getting married? What if the Lord returns before I get married? Ever had those thoughts rattle you?

In the silence of yet another dateless weekend have you heard the insistent ticking of the biological time clock and your mother's admonition, "Don't wait too late!" Ark thinking leads some people to say premature or unwise "I do's" that lead to hellish existences and to second-class living as married adults. Look back at Genesis 2:18, "It is not good for the man to be alone." Can't you name some married people who are alone emotionally or spiritually?

The loneliest person in your zip code last night wasn't a single adult, but a married adult, lying on his side of the bed thinking, *O God, when is it ever going to get better?*

I think of a missionary who went to Africa and gave forty years of faithful service, then came home to retire. Without a family, she dreaded retirement. She found a small apartment in a retirement complex in Southern California. She discovered a colleague, a recent widower, from early in her missionary career.

During those long years in Africa, she assumed that marriage had been forever ruled out. She thought her *yes* to God's best squelched any "I do's."

However, on God's agenda, marriage was the pleasant surprise He had planned for this faithful servant. She fell in love and married. Today that couple is one of the happiest that I know. Was she deprived all those years? Was she a "half-person"?

One million years from now, how will she view that mere season of singleness? That moment in eternity when she will bring Africans as her love gift to the Saviour, will she lament her singleness?

Jesus frees us from *ark* thinking so that we can pursue the abundant life.

JESUS FREES SINGLES FROM ASH THINKING

We live in an age of success obsession. Everyone wants to be a success. Walk into a B. Dalton's bookstore. Success is apparent in the titles of many popular books. Ask, "Do you have a book on failure?" and watch the clerk's reaction. Who buys all the success books? Failures.

I am on a committee planning an international conference and we want speakers who can challenge the delegates. I suggested a well-known author whose bestseller on success I had just read. One of the committee members interrupted.

"We tried to get him, but he charges $10,000 for one speech."

That's not bad for an hour's work. I doubt that he spends weeks preparing for one particular lecture. Moreover, I doubt that he has anything new to say (he's saving that for the sequel).

I predict that in one year there will be another new star of success on the scene for those who failed the current star's system.

Jesus looks across our lives and sees our failures. Think of Hannah, Samuel's mother, who lived under *ark* thinking. For years she struggled with her infertility and the whispers of her neighbors.

Finally, out of necessity, her husband took another wife, Peninnah. She taunted Hannah and mocked her. Peninnah's pregnancy proved Hannah to be the source of the infertility rather than the husband.

Year after year Hannah journeyed to Shiloh. She would see women there who had gotten pregnant since the previous festival. She would hear the "oohs and ahs" that "so-and-so is pregnant" and "after all these years!"

Then we find Hannah, "in bitterness of soul" weeping "much and [praying] to the Lord" (1 Sam. 1:10). She wanted a child to fulfill her role as a woman. Eli, the priest, mistook Hannah's motive and scolded, "How long will you keep getting drunk? Get rid of your wine" (v. 14).

Some of us know what ashes smell and taste like. We have lain in the ashes. Our worlds, our charred dreams have lain crumbled around us. It may have been a divorce, the death of a mate, a broken engagement, a job loss. Whatever—we have felt the hot singe of the embers.

As a child, I had the chore of burning trash in an old oil barrel. I loved that job. Watching things burn fascinated me. But my chore had one drawback: I always smelled like smoke. Sometimes today I smell the scent of failure when talking with some single adults.

Many of us learned about Hannah in Sunday School through the stories of Samuel, the son she presented to the Lord. She presented her son to the same priest who had falsely accused her of being drunk. But the son God gave her wasn't just any son. Samuel became the spiritual giant of Israel.

Before Samuel, the Israelities were twelve tribes—each doing their own thing. Samuel, however, molded them into a people, ruled by a monarchy. All history has beeninfluenced by that boy's life.

No wonder the Word declares:

> He raises the poor from the dust and lifts the needy from the ash heap; He seats them with princes and has them inherit a throne of honor (1 Sam. 2:8).

Later, David added, knowing the entire story, "He settles the barren woman in her home as a happy mother of children" (Ps. 113:9). David had been anointed King of Israel by the son of a barren woman.

What about Jesus' words on abundant living? Do you feel that you cannot live an abundant life after what has happened to you or after what you've been through?

Jesus comes to us in the midst of our messes, our tragedies, our dilemmas. Our theology, in order to be valid, has to work in the midst of our messes. Our God is the One who calls us to abandon our ash heaps.

In the ashes of yesterday you can find the nutrients for tomorrow's dreams. At the University of the South, a brilliant professor's son was killed. This theologian was so devastated that he couldn't teach his classes. Weeks passed. Then one night he showed up at a faculty banquet and asked if he could say a few words.

"In the last few weeks," he began, "I have been to the bottom. But," he paused, "I am happy to report that the bottom is solid!"

The dean of the seminary, reflecting on the banquet, later observed, "God is in the garbage of my life just as much as in the competence. Our lives are like a parfait glass. Yes, there is that lower layer but there are those upper layers too."[5]

Jesus frees us from *ash* thinking so that we can pursue the abundant life.

JESUS FREES SINGLES FROM APE THINKING

Jesus frees us from *ape* thinking. Americans are fascinated by "the latest." Have you heard the latest? Have you read the latest? We live in an age of instant communication. A TV evangelist can sneeze and 100,000 people will simultaneously say, "Gesundheit!"

Truth can be transmitted in an instant. Yet, so can heresy.

Though heresy may be corrected "in the next broadcast," thousands will have already quoted it and believed it.

We are authority-conscious. "Says who?" we demand. Celebrity conscious and hungry for heroes, some of us will overlook inconsistencies in our favorite performers' lives and lifestyles.

U.S. News and World Report published an article, "Heroes Are Back" noting that in the 1970s heroes were in short supply. People had difficulty finding a public figure they liked let alone admired. One study conducted by the Roper Organization found that young adults "tend to choose strong individuals as their models and clearly seek to pattern themselves after people, who, for the most part, are *boundlessly rich or successful*" (italics added). Look at their choices (participants could make more than one choice):

1.	Clint Eastwood, actor	(30%)
2.	Eddie Murphy, actor	(24%)
3.	Ronald Reagan, President	(15%)
4.	Jane Fonda, actress/fitness entrepreneur	(14.3%)
5.	Sally Field, actress	(13.7%)
	Stephen Spielberg, movie producer	(13.7%)
7.	John Paul II, Pope	(17%)
8.	Mother Theresa, humanitarian	(10%)
9.	Michael Jackson, songwriter	(9.5%)
	Tina Turner, soul and rock singer	(9.5%)[6]

However, one significant statistic was that 19 percent or one in five surveyed had "no hero or heroines."

Evangelicals have been almost as hungry for celebrities. *Guess who just got saved?* is a common question. Actors, politicians, drug dealers, and athletes make popular new Christians. Mike Yaconelli, in an article titled, "Thou Shall Have No Other Celebrities before Me," lamented:

> The media can only capture moments in people's lives but too often we take those moments and compare them to the *total* moments of our lives. The result is that we can't imagine Billy Graham getting angry (or even annoyed) at his wife; we can't comprehend Chuck Swindoll having a bad

> day; we can't fathom Karen Mains yelling at her kids.
>
> We compare the perfections of these celebrities to our imperfections and we get discouraged or worse yet, we put the celebrity on a pedestal and expect them to have all the answers to all of life's problems.[6]

Thus, in the age of the electronic church, "we refuse to give up our worship of the celebrity."[7]

> There seems to be this . . . longing to hope with all our hearts that someone is able to live this Christian life the way it is supposed to be lived. We can't live that way, but surely Chuck Swindoll or Amy Grant or Joni can. Please God tell us it's true.[8]

The second consequence of *ape* thinking is that the media makes everyone an instant expert, pop theologian, or social commentator "anxious to share a word" or two.

Ape thinkers offer 1, 2, 3's and instant solutions. "You've got a problem, huh? Well, here's the solution, brother!" Chuck Colson reminds us that Jesus taught in parables, but

> We tend to think we have to go into lengthy, detailed, elaborate explanations with eighteen steps. Or we go to the other extreme which is to reduce things to simple formulas. There is a mysticism to our faith which we can't simply formulize.[9]

So, we race to the next seminar, listen to the next cassette or book, read the next article, make the next speaker, "it." We put him or her up there on a pedestal. But no matter who puts the speaker up there, according to Bob Benson, there's only one way down![10] *Ape* thinking grafts worldly attitudes onto our faith. Colson contends, "The Gospel is not a message of self-gratification. It is a message of self-giving."[11]

Gary Collins offers an alternative. Single adults must:

> stop wasting time trying to integrate biblical teaching with these systems that offer so little promise. Instead, let us join in the intensive, excitingly fresh study of the Scriptures in relation to human problems and needs.[12]

How many single adults are looking for "Cliff Notes" rather than immersing themselves in the Word? No wonder we fall victim to what Wayne Oates termed "pack thinkers" who think only along "party lines."[13] I still expect to pick up the paper and read the headline:

Single Killed By Original Thought!

In today's world, it is so easy to be an *ape* thinker. Many remain spiritual infants, "tossed back and forth by the waves, and blown here and there by every wind of teaching" (Eph. 4:14). We are captivated by the new—whether it is a deodorant or a doctrine. Heresy becomes acceptable to people too busy to think for themselves.

We need to be like the Bereans described in the Book of Acts. "They received the message with great eagerness" (there's nothing wrong with enthusiasm). They "examined the Scriptures *every day* to see if what Paul said was true" (Acts 17:11).

What? If they actually challenged Paul, the greatest missionary, Then how much more do we need to challenge current speakers? To test their words against the Word?

Russell Dilday, president of Southwestern Seminary, said "Trivial pursuit is more than a game. It is a tragic description of the lives of so many of our day . . . who give their lives to that which is not important.[14]

Jesus frees us from *ape* thinking so that we can pursue the abundant life.

JESUS FREES SINGLES FROM ASK THINKING

"Ask and it will be given to you" (Matt. 7:7).

"Amen, I *like* that verse," respond many single adults.

Some have taken that verse and twisted it into heresy. We want more to boost our faith and help us take those giant steps. Thus, Jesus, in the process, has become the cosmic, eternal Santa Claus. The divine Neiman-Marcus catalog. The head of our heavenly room service.

Prayer for many single adults means, "Give me." A few singles teach that if they use a certain word, a code phrase,

God will grant their requests quicker. Some think they have to "talk God into it."

Tragically, according to Oswald Chambers, singles look upon prayer as "a means of getting things." Rather, the biblical idea is "that we may get to know God Himself."[15] Jesus' life illustrates this point. Jesus already had it all. Still, He spent nights in prayer, communicating with His Father.

The prosperity gospel is attractive and seductive: "God wants *you* rich and prosperous!" It's taught with pep rally enthusiasm. "Three cheers for God!" Prosperity gospel is in essence a Madison Avenue version of the old puritan work ethic.

So, God wants His children rich and prosperous? What about those poor single adult Christians in Africa? Doesn't God care about them? Does He love *us* more than them? Wouldn't they like to have air-conditioned, fully loaded BMWs to cut through the desert, looking for food or firewood or water?

The Word says, "Give, and it will be given to you" (Luke 6:38). Many single adults have concluded that their spiritual gift is *receiving*. No way—it's giving! For when we give, we receive "a good measure, pressed down, shaken together and running over. . . . With the measure you use, it will be measured to you" (v. 38).

God is concerned about our needs, but not necessarily our wants or those needs which have resulted from greed. It's hard to whine to God about your $800 Visa bill. Rich American single adults (compared to the world standard) must learn, perhaps through economic trauma, to live more simply so that others can simply live.

One single snapped, "I refuse to feel guilty about my prosperity!" I understand that to a degree, but God allows prosperity so that you can pour it out and give it away. God wants to bless you to bless others. You are to be a conduit through which His resources flow to answer prayer.

Jesus frees us from *ask* thinking so that we can pursue the abundant life.

CONCLUSION

Jesus calls every single adult to the abundant lifestyle. There are no lone rangers, no individuals—just members of one body. He invites you to come follow Him, to experience the abundance.

How many single adults have defined abundant living as the American dream with my initials on it: spouse, 2.3 kids, new car, PTA, scouts, two weeks vacation, sporadic ski weekends, microwaves, VCR, personal computer, miscellaneous electronic gadgets, etc.

But what has abundant living meant to single adults?

To May Smith, abundant living meant helping newborn babies survive. It meant founding the Dallas Babies Hospital in tents borrowed from the Red Cross and pitched on the lawn of the Parkland General Hospital.

To Liz Bailey, a widow, abundant living meant continuing the giggling laughter of children at a circus. When her husband died, she kept the circus on the road.

To Donaldina Cameron, abundant living meant rescuing teenage Chinese girls from brothels in San Francisco.

To Dag Hammarskjold, abundant living meant giving his life to a peace-keeping organization; it meant dying in the Congo trying to bring order to a hot spot.

To thousands of other kingdom-seekers, abundant living has meant opportunities to give significant chunks of themselves without reservation. The same Jesus that enabled them will enable you.

Jesus accomplished the impossible. He freed and *frees* us from *ark, ash, ape,* and *ask* thinking.

A crucial agenda of adulthood is what will you do with the call of Jesus? Will you accept His invitation to enjoy that abundant living?

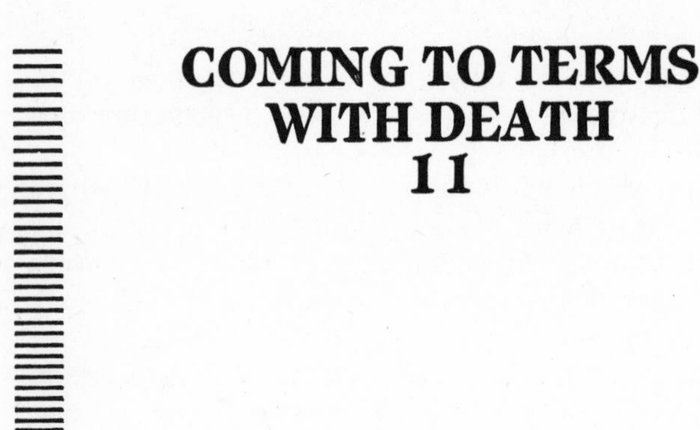

COMING TO TERMS WITH DEATH
11

There's always one part of my introduction as a speaker that gets a laugh: "Our speaker is a graduate of the Kentucky School of Mortuary Science."

Some in the audience assume it is a joke. Afterward, people ask, "Were you really an undertaker?"

The last thing most single adults want to think about is death (and it is the last thing they *will* think about). Americans will go to any length to disguise death. We call *mortuaries* "funeral homes"; *undertakers* are "funeral directors." We seldom say anyone is *dead,* but "gone" or "with the Lord."

Even with my mortuary science background, I was not prepared for the visits I made to the San Diego cemetery in 1978. Just seven months before, the president of the college for which I worked had been diagnosed as having cancer. Yet, that day he stood not far from me. We were there for the funeral of a Point Loma College student—the third student who died that year. I recall his remarks after the first death. "You were so busy praying for me that you failed to pray for Becky" (who had been killed in an avalanche during the Christmas holiday break). "None of us dreamed that Becky would die before me." He pointed out that each student had an appointment; some sooner than others.

At that third memorial service, the college chaplain confessed, "If I knew what to say, I'd say it. If I knew what to sing, I'd sing it."

We had said everything that we had ever heard—especially those trite mumblings we offer at funeral homes. Somebody needed to think of something fresh.

DEATH IS A REALITY

Jewish proverbs explain our skepticism. "Every man knows he will die; but no man wants to believe it!" Or, "Life is only loaned to us; death is the creditor who will one day collect." Most of us look at death in light of statistics. The numbers show that the six primary causes of death are:

Cardiovascular disease:	424.2 per 100,000 population
Cancer:	184.0 per 100,000
Accidents:	43.9 per 100,000
Pulmonary diseases:	25.7 per 100,000
Diabetes:	15.1 per 100,000
Homicide:	10.3 per 100,000[1]

Ironically, the leading cause of death is *life*.

Gail Howard noted, "I am afraid—not scared of dying—but of living"[2] Our only consolation, however, with the three college students was that they had already tasted of the abundant life. None was waiting until graduation for life to begin. "After all," Scott Peck observed, "Jesus is not so concerned with the length of life as with its vitality."[3] The length of "our playing time" is known only to God. "Man is destined to die once, and after that to face judgment" (Heb. 9:27).

The mature single adult must say, "I am learning to accept my own mortality."

DEATH IS A NECESSITY

In a sermon entitled, "Death: More Friend than Foe," William Sloane Coffin suggested if you don't like death, consider the alternatives.

> Life without death would be interminable—both literally and figuratively. We would take weeks just to get out of bed, weeks to decide what to do

> next . . . meetings would drag on for months. . . . Put differently, just as without leave-taking there can be no arrival; just as without growing old, there can be no growing up; just as without tears, no laughter; so without death, there could be no living.[4]

God did a merciful thing by introducing death. What if Adam and Eve were still alive today? Tormented by the obvious consequences of their disobedience? Think of so many people, prisoners of sorts to their own bodies, imprisoned by life-support (actually death-avoidance) technology. Are they testimonies to modern science? Or evidence of man's inability to face death?

During the time of dying of our college president, one church member in the college church celebrated his 100th birthday. "What is your birthday wish?" our pastor asked.

"To go home . . . to be with Jesus," he responded.

To die? How ironic! A man wanting to die was forced to wait out his tardy death angel while our president courageously fought off his.

Death is the ultimate rest for our bodies. But that doesn't help us accept the death of the young. Early in life we learn, "There are only two things you can't escape: death and taxes."

DEATH IS A CERTAINTY

Jesus enjoyed a close relationship with three single adults: Mary, Martha, and Lazarus. When Lazarus became ill, his sisters naturally sent word to Jesus, "Lord, the one You love is sick." Apparently, they assumed their message, so emotionally coded, would cause Jesus to rearrange His schedule. Hardly. "He stayed where He was for two more days" (John 11:6).

By the time Jesus arrived, Lazarus had been dead for four days. Many Jews from Jerusalem had come to Bethany to comfort the two single sisters. In a day without Social Security, welfare, and pensions, with little recognition of the status of women, these ladies faced a crisis.

Jesus' action (or inaction) wounded both women. "Lord, if You had been here," Martha scolded, "my brother would not have died" (v. 21). Later, Mary repeated the accusation, perhaps more pathetically since John noted, "She fell at His feet" (v. 32). Her action (as well as that of the Jewish mourners) "deeply moved" yet "troubled" Jesus.

Confronting death was a necessary part of His apprenticeship with life. He had already faced down death with the resurrection of the widow of Nain's son. But that was a stranger's grief. Now He experienced the death of a friend; He grieved.

Jesus was affected by Mary's tears—her grief. Thus, "Jesus wept" (v. 35).

Jesus did not weep over the death of Lazarus. Rather, He wept at the sisters' lack of understanding of death and who He was. It was not until verse 38 that Jesus "came to the tomb."

Jesus knew death was a certainty and the death of Lazarus and his resurrection gave Jesus a firsthand encounter with death.

DEATH IS AN OPPORTUNITY

How can I say that death is *an opportunity?* For pain? For suffering? Each of us—regardless of age, sex, or marital status—must face three categories of death:

- parents or family members
- significant others
- ourselves

Some of our attitudes toward death are shaped when we are too young to understand let alone express our fears. My early encounter with death came at age six. My father worked for the Louisville Gas and Electric Company. Death was a daily potential threat. How many times did our household become silent when a radio announcer said: "An unidentified LG&E employee has been electrocuted." Like "police" families, we waited for the phone call or knock at the door.

When my dad took his vacation, his friend Bruce Roddenkamp took his place as gang foreman. Bruce was electrocuted the week of Dad's vacation in a freak accident.

At the funeral home, I remember clinging tightly to my dad's legs as he offered his condolences to the young widow. Then he said to me, "Say something to Jimmy."

I stood eye-to-eye with the dead man's son, but I couldn't say, "I'm sorry." My dad even coached the words and grew irritated with me. Fortunately, the widow understood.

Jimmy came back to school a week later. When we put our heads down at nap time. I twisted so I could watch him. Most of the time, he just stared out the window; sometimes he cried quietly.

I couldn't tell him that I was sorry. In my six-year-old mind, I concluded that if it hadn't been *his* dad, it would have been *mine*. Worse were the nightmares. My parents didn't understand my grief. I didn't have a vocabularly to explain my terror.

Frederick Beuchner, the writer, recalled his early encounter with death:

> On a Saturday in late fall, my brother and I woke up around sunrise. I was ten and he was not quite eight, and once we were awake there was no going back to sleep. . . . Our mother and father were going to take us to a football game, and although we were not particularly interested in the game, we were desperately interested in being taken. . . . It was much too early to get up, so we amused ourselves as best we could until the rest of the house got moving.
>
> While the two boys played
>
> our bedroom door opened a little, and somebody looked in on us. It was our father. . . . There was apparently nothing about his appearance or about what he said or did that made us look twice at him. There was nothing to suggest that he opened the door for any reason other than to check on us as he passed by on his way to the bathroom or whatever else we might have thought he was going to do on

> a Saturday morning. . . . I have no idea of how long he stood there looking at us. A few seconds? A few minutes? Did he smile, make a face, wave his hand? I have no idea. All I know is that after a while, he disappeared closing the door behind him, and we went on playing.[5]

Beuchner explained, "That brief moment was the last of my childhood. For the world came to an end that Saturday morning." Buechner's father committed suicide as the boys played. And a ten-year-old was left to wonder *Why?*

I think that to those of us who are unmarried and do not have children, the death of our parents—at whatever age—can be more difficult to accept; more threatening. Historically, the unmarried have been held more responsible for the care of aging parents. Some women, in fact, have seen opportunities for marriage pass them by while they took care of their parents.

Henry Nouwen wrote that the hardest thing about his mother's death was driving home from the hospital.

> When we turned into the road leading to our house, I suddenly felt a deep, inner sadness. Tears came to my eyes and I did not dare to look at my father. We both understood. She would not be home. She would not open the door and embrace us. She would not ask how the day had been. She would not invite us to the table and pour tea in our cups.[6]

The other side was a glorious reality that never again would his mother be sick or in pain.

It is also difficult to accept the death of a friend or colleague. Mary Randolph, Director of Single Adults at Asbury Park United Methodist Church in Tulsa, helped her group rally around two dying men. The first, a young doctor, decided to fight to at least finish his internship. When his wife left him, he found hope in Mary's single adult group. He soon began teaching a Bible study; no moping around for him.

One night, however, it was obvious that he was in great

wracking pain. Finally, one of the group members interrupted, "Would it be all right if we just stopped and held you?"

This tall young doctor received a comfort that was beyond comprehension. Six months before, this group had been strangers. Now they proved the accuracy of the psalmist: "God sets the lonely in families" (Ps. 68:6).

Mary also described another young man—alienated from his family. His pain, anger, and lack of social skills made it difficult for the group to love him. Yet, the group accepted him as he was. His nonchurched family was stunned by the number of singles who attended his funeral. "We didn't know he had this many friends!"

Moreover, neither man has been forgotten.

I have a friend who is a hospice counselor and works with a lot of single adults. I asked, "How do you deal with it?"

"I cry a lot," he responded.

After one funeral he explained, "I was flooded with feelings of my friend's *specialness*. I remembered him telling me that the hardest part of dying was 'seeing the sorrow in your friends, eyes.' "

This counselor concluded, "We must embrace life (and death) as a process of becoming more, not less. Once we can accept and let go of our resistance to death, we can approach each moment as a possibility."[7]

Another worker commented, "I thought I would be helping people die. Instead, I'm learning how to live."

We must also confront our own death. Jesus in His struggle chose those closest to Him to help with this ordeal. Take a close look at the descriptions of His death struggle.

> He began to be sorrowful and troubled. Then He said to them, "My soul is overwhelmed with sorrow to the point of death. Stay here and keep watch with Me" (Matt. 26:37-38).
>
> Jesus "fell to the ground and prayed. . . . 'Take this cup from Me' " (Mark 14:35-36).

> In anguish, He prayed more earnestly, and His sweat was like drops of blood falling to the ground (Luke 22:44).

His moanings hardly phased the steady snoozing of the three trusted disciples. Rather "an angel from heaven . . . strengthened Him," not those He loved the most (Luke 22:43).

How do we confront our own death? Maybe it is a gift of sorts to know it is coming. To have time to "put our affairs in order" or to say our "good-byes."

One young cancer patient explained:

> All my philosophies—and I've had a lot of them—about what death is—have gone down the drain. When you're facing the stark reality of things, you find you look at them in a different way.[8]

A clinical psychologist, a single parent, dying at age forty-six, noted:

> In the aftermath of the most severe dislocations of my forty-six years, I find myself able to weather the storms with fortifying doses of humor, screaming fits . . . crying, and the support of children and loving friends. My friends have opened their arms to me in ways that before they hadn't.

He continued:

> Impending death is a reality for us all. But to me it has become far less important to dwell on that fact than to address the tragedy of living life burdened with fears, lies, or indifference in all the stunning variety of forms that these take—like perpetuating a negative self-image, doing a job that one hates, *or making oneself hostage to the rules of the jungle at the expense of all else in life.*[9]

I know what you're thinking. Married couples can help each other and be there for each other when their moments of death approach. But as a single, you may feel that you have no one you can turn to at such a time. When you come down to put your toe in the chilly tide of Jordan, who will be there for you?

Donald Catalino and Colleen Leahy Johnson have studied the support systems of the "childless elderly." Though children are often described as one's old—age insurance, Catalino and Johnson discovered that the childless unmarried are more likely than married people to be involved with kin. Singles usually have developed broader "networks of interaction and reciprocity." Married couples have traditionally relied on each other to meet their needs; many do not want to burden their children. But the death of one wipes out the support system of the other.[10]

The unmarried, however, across the years have built up a stockpile of resources in some type of extended family and friends in expectation of the possibility of dependency. Married people have generally worked to *exclude* others while singles have worked to *include*. The research found special relationships between single adults and nieces or nephews which had been nurtured across the years.

Thus, Catalino and Johnson concluded that single adults are better prepared to face the triumvirate: retirement, old age, and death. Singles over the years

> have adopted the role model of the autonomous, independent person who remains engaged in a network of friends and relatives. Consequently, the transition into dependency in old age has been rehearsed and resources are likely to be more available.[11]

Consider a widower who must now wash or cook for himself. He was probably used to gender-specific behaviors (such jobs were women's work). What about the widow facing house or automobile repairs? The researchers discovered singles are "usually more resourceful in dealing with losses psychologically and socially."[12]

There is yet another dimension to this opportunity. That is closure. Elisabeth Kubler-Ross observed that for someone who has not first loved, death always comes too soon! But for those who have worked through their priorities, "death becomes one more adventure and discovery."[13] That sounds insane. Yet the Christian repeats Paul's words, "Where, O

Death, is your victory? Where, O Death, is your sting?" Paul declared confidently, "Thanks be to God! He gives *us* the victory through our Lord Jesus Christ" (1 Cor. 15:55, 57).

Vice President Hubert Humphrey, dying with cancer, called his long-time political enemy, Richard Nixon—the man who had narrowly defeated him for the presidency in 1968. When skeptics asked why, Humphrey explained that at death's door some things looked differently than before.

Many single adults are trying to negotiate treaties with death. One man noted:

> Death leaves our hierachy of priorities a sham. Long hours in committee meetings, night after night at the office, scrambling to meet the payments on a new house, the constant anticipation of a promotion. What does it all amount to now? Would you do it all over again if you had the chance?[14]

Dying is a time to mend family relationships. Consider the hatred between Isaac and Ishmael. When Abraham, their father, died "at a good old age. . . . His sons Isaac *and* Ishmael buried him" (Gen. 25:7, 9). Consider the strain between Jacob and Esau. Yet when Isaac died at 185 years, "his sons Esau *and* Jacob buried him" (35:28-29).

CAN I TAKE ADVANTAGE OF AN OPPORTUNITY THAT I DON'T WANT?

Remember, death really is not optional. The consequence of life is death. But here are some helpful suggestions:

1. *Confront your fears.* Doug Manning encourages this in *Don't Take Away My Grief.* Jesus mourned for His cousin, John the Baptist. Other Bible heroes also expressed their grief. (Jesus—John 11:33-35; Abraham—Gen 23:1-3; Isaac—Gen. 24:67; Jacob—Gen. 3:35; Joseph—Gen. 50:1).

2. *Aim for something that will make a difference.* Manning insists that there are two important days in everyone's life: the day we are born and the day we discover *why* we were born.[15] It would be a tragedy to die before you made that discovery. I like this anonymous verse:

THAT SINGLE IS A SUCCESS
who has lived well, laughed often and loved much;
who has gained the respect of intelligent men and
the love of children;
who has filled his niche and accomplished his task;
who leaves the world better than he found it,
whether by an improved poppy, a perfect poem,
or a rescued soul;
who never lacked appreciation of earth's beauty or
failed to express it;
who looked for the best in others and gave the best
all he had.

3. *Befriend death.* One way I began befriending death was by drawing up a will, carefully selecting ministries that will share whatever estate I have accumulated. That money will be in circulation long after my checking account has been closed.

Buy a cemetery lot. Make your funeral arrangments.

4. *Determine to die with dignity.* I do not want to have my life prolonged to be a statistic on some graph in a medical journal. Charles Meyer lamented, "In the past, death came and little could be done to hold it back. This is no longer true."[14] Technology can keep us in its custody."[16]

Discuss your attitude toward life-support systems with your primary-care physician. Do you want to be placed on them? Now is the time to make him aware of your preferences.

DEATH IS A BEGINNING

Science has raced far ahead of theology. Because we deify physicians in our culture, they are calling all the shots. But death is primarily a theological issue. Though it is a biological ending, it is a spiritual beginning.

As she lay dying, missionary leader Belle Bennett reminded her friends, "There is one inflexible sphere and that is old age which God in mercy breaks with the hammer of death."[17] Death was but another chapter in the courageous life of this great woman.

D.L. Moody underlined this concept.

> By and by you will hear people say, "Mr. Moody is dead!" Don't believe a word of it. At that *very* moment, I shall be more alive than I am now. I shall *then* begin to live.[18]

Paul reminded us that "to be absent from the body" is to "be present with the Lord" (2 Cor. 5:8, KJV). *The Book of Common Prayer* asks, "What do we mean by everlasting life?"

> By everlasting life, we mean a *new* existence, in which we are united with all the people of God, in the joy of fully knowing God and each other.[17]

Part of our problem is that singles are so scientifically oriented. We dissect things or place them under microscopes or feed the data into computers. It's difficult for us to accept Jesus' promise, "I am going there to prepare a place for *you*. And if I go and prepare a place for you, I will come back and take you to be with Me that you also may be where I am" (John 14:2-3). William Coffin explained, "I may not understand the what of eternity but I do trust the who."[20]

A single adult named Gail Howard commented:

> I really don't think of heaven so much as a place of rest and golden streets, as I think of it as a place where I can serve God unshackled from my present limitations of finiteness which so often get in the way.[21]

Death is only the beginning. God is committed to the best for His children. He has devised death for the Christian to be merely the doorway through which we enter into His presence.

CONCLUSION

One of the last agenda items for single adults is coming to terms with death and dying: of our family members, of significant others, and of ourselves. The time to deal with that reality is *now*. Tragically, too many single adults postpone it and then struggle with those "I wish I had said's."

Norbert Elias reminds us that death is only a problem for the living. "Dead people have no problems." But we of all the creatures on this earth "know that we shall die; we alone can anticipate our own end."[22] Therefore we can do something about it, today. Gail Howard asks:

> If you knew death was coming tomorrow, would it make you any less afraid to do the things you were afraid to do today?
>
> Perhaps we need the kind of belief that gives the courage to be the person we would be knowing that today is the *last* time on earth we would be given the opportunity to communicate our love to others.[23]

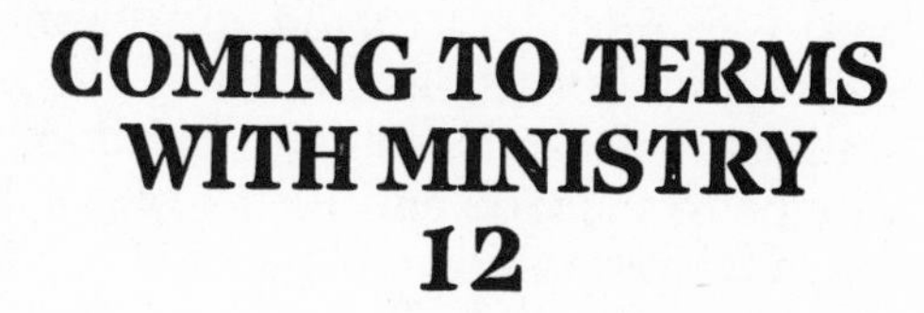

COMING TO TERMS WITH MINISTRY 12

What does it mean to be Christian and single? John Donne penned that classic phrase, "No man is an island." We have a commitment to one another. The Apostle Paul insisted, "For none of us lives to himself, and no man dies to himself. For whether we live, we live unto the Lord, and whether we die, we die unto the Lord: whether we live therefore, or die, we are the Lord's" (Rom. 14:7-8, KJV).

Dietrich Bonhoeffer, a single adult German theologian, stated, "God has willed that we should seek and find His living word in the witness of a brother." The single adult, he concluded, "needs another Christian who speaks God's Word to him."[1]

We must share our knowledge of faith and discipline with others. Yet, most of us are hesitant—perhaps afraid—to witness. Bonhoeffer asked:

> Why should we be afraid of one another, since both of us have only God to fear? Why should we think that our brother would not understand us, when we understood very well what was meant when somebody spoke God's comfort or God's admonition to us, perhaps in words that were halting and unskilled?[2]

When we confront or comfort a single adult, we recognize his dignity and humanity. He will be "lonely and lost" if not given help. Life resembles a road map. Sometimes we need someone to point out landmarks. Every single adult has a right to abundant life and positive singlehood. Paul explained: "Praise be to the God and Father of our Lord Jesus Christ, the Father of compassion and the God of all comfort." Well, that sounds good. But Paul continued, "who comforts us . . . *so that* we can comfort those in any trouble with the comfort we ourselves have received from God" (2 Cor. 1:3-4).

Some would reject the equation of "any trouble" in this passage with singleness. The reality, however, is clear to anyone who has is single or who has listened to singles.

Many singles are hamstrung by a poor self-image. To some the word *single* is as offensive as a racial slur. "I'm *not* single!" they protest. Some have built high walls around their spirits to discourage penetration. "I'm never going to be hurt again." So they live in a self-designed prison. In *Warm Reflections* I wrote:

I am alone!
I have accepted my aloneness.
I have not cursed it,
    nor have I welcomed it for a prolonged visit.
At this point I choose to be hospitable
    rather than face a duel.
Aloneness is an abstraction,
    a coloring-book word,
    and the coloration I choose to grant it
    will define whether I become
        a *warden* to aloneness
        or merely a *prisoner*.[3]

There is a need for a positive model of spiritual vitality among single adults that would not glorify an individual but exalt Christ, the enabling power. Paul's imprisonment did not depress his colleagues but encouraged them. "Because of my chains, most of the brothers in the Lord have been encouraged to speak the word of God more courageously and fearlessly" (Phil. 1:14).

Single adults need to support one another. It is OK to be single. Singleness can be good—if we choose to make it so. Supposedly, the grass is greener on the other side of the fence. But it is always greener where it is watered!

We cannot be theological lone rangers among singles. There are too many who have tried that route—stalking singledom on their white horses. Cain snapped at God, "Am I my brother's keeper?" (Gen. 4:9) The answer then and now is, "yes!" Paul insisted that we bear "one another's burdens, and so fulfill the law of Christ" (Gal. 6:2, KJV). May I add, *even when you do not feel like it or it is inconvenient.* "The brother is a brother to the Christian, precisely because he is a Christian." A non-Christian merely sidesteps every burden or inconvenience.[4]

The purpose of ministry is not to replace the singles' bar or provide "spiritual" entertainment or distraction from the problems of being single. A singles' group must be more than someplace to go and/or something to do to fill in empty hours on a social calendar. Tragically, in an attempt to gather members, too many programs have stressed entertainment; program rather than ministry.

The world does a better job entertaining. Yet, we are often afraid that secular single adults will not listen or that they will reject us or make fun. Why would they want to go to a church gathering when they could go to Rasputin's or the Brass Rail or the Scoreboard?

Peter wrote, "Always be prepared to give an answer to everyone who asks you to give the reason for the hope that you have. But do this with gentleness and respect" (1 Peter 3:15). I had a friend who thought everyone was going to hell. *Everything* was wrong or sinful. He thought his ministry was "setting people straight." This Mork-like character spoke another language than most of the residents of his apartment complex. He had difficulty understanding why he was such an ineffective witness. Why his neighbors always examined his words for the telltale fingerprints of judgment.

Often we resist sharing our witness because our celibacy is such a contrast to the sexual mores or the estimation of what sexual conduct is today. "They will think I'm crazy or gay—everyone sleeps around." Yet, it was Dr. Gabrielle Brown's *The New Celibacy,* a secular book, that made the bestseller lists and contradicted that notion.[5]

I am a Christian. I do not feel any less a male because of my faith. My lifestyle is not based on Eastern mysticism or self-righteous self-discipline. Jesus modeled complete, abundant, and meaningful singlehood. Single adults can gain such strength from His example and still not have to flee to a monastery.

We are called to be witnesses so that singles may see (and not only hear) our testimonies. Hebrews 12:1 mentions the "men of faith watching from the heavenly grandstands": "Wherefore seeing we also are compassed about with so great a cloud of witnesses, let us lay aside every weight, and the sin which does so easily beset us, and let us run with patience the race that is set before us" (KJV).

I believe that verse has some validity to those who carefully watch our lives here. Single men hear what you profess in church and what you confess in the locker room. Singles compare your witness on Sunday morning with your lifestyle on Saturday night.

While there are sins which trip and trap, the enemy gets too much credit. *The devil made me do it* is so convenient an excuse. Some singles sabotage themselves. Some of us covet the expensive sports car, the glittery jewelry, the prestigious condo or address, or even the "successful" single who seems to have everything going for him. As a result, we curse our singleness (and sometimes ourselves) and live for that tomorrow when we will meet SOMEONE and fall in love and get married. How easily we put our ministry "on hold" until Prince or Princess Charming shows up.

Realistically, anything that keeps us from living fully Christian lives in whatever status—married or single—is sin. Too many singles live with the constant thought *if I were only married, then. . . .* Ironically, there is nothing about saying *I do* that suddenly ignites our ministry gifts.

Our generation stakes everything on personal happiness

and immediate gratification. Thus, we have become so possession-conscious that we have become isolated. The phrase "which does so easily beset us" from Hebrews 12:1 is not accidental. Too many of us are limited not by circumstances, but rather by our responses to events which happen to us. Maximilian Kolbe and Corrie ten Boom, two single adults imprisoned in concentration camps by the Nazis, refused to give the Nazis the total say on their confinement. Both heroically chose to *respond* rather than *react* to their situations.

Most of us believe that we have a right to feel the way we do. Too easily some assume the martyr's badge of loneliness. However, Scripture warns us not to be "conformed" to this world but to be "transformed by the renewing of your mind" (Rom. 12:2, KJV) and our attitudes. Successful single living is dependent upon positive attitudes toward self, status, and others. And these attitudes do not develop overnight.

The question is not how to survive singleness long enough to get married. But how do I enjoy my singleness now? Proverbs suggest, "Let your manhood be a blessing" (5:18, TLB). We could paraphrase that, "Let your SINGLENESS be a blessing."

When the Israelites were taken captive, they wept. They remembered all that was no longer a part of their lifestyle. Their captors, having heard of the Jews' musical talents, demanded a song. The Jews responded, "How can we sing the songs of the Lord while in a foreign land?" (Ps. 137: 3-4) Some have read that passage and concluded that the captors were teasing them; others see in the request an opportunity. Similarly, some secular single adults want to hear our song.

How do we sing the Lord's song when we did not have a date last week—or cannot remember the last good date we had? When we thought a relationship was developing and found the other person was not as interested? How do we sing the Lord's song of triumphant single living in a world of sexual anarchy? How do we sing the Lord's song:

Confidently?
Conspicuously?
Compassionately?

We can look beyond ourselves to others. We can look beyond our hurts and loneliness to the needs of others. Too many activities are "time taker-uppers" or distractions from our problems. But if we could see our problems as opportunities, we would find many occasions for ministry.

THE MINISTRY OF HOLDING ONE'S TONGUE

James declared, "No man can tame the tongue" (James 3:8). We judge, scrutinize, and condemn other singles who fail to meet our expectations. We self-righteously appoint ourselves to put some single adults "in their place." Some singles have taken upon themselves to define for everyone what is the proper standard on any subject. And woe to anyone who does not believe as they do!

Part of "holding one's tongue" is to give other single adults a chance. How often when we meet a stranger in a singles' group do we give him the "once-over" to see if he is going to threaten our position? Singles' groups, particularly in small churches, can become cliques. Too often we expect members to conform to our agendas. To be like us. The purpose of single adult groups is not to mass-produce single adults who walk alike, think alike, are alike. It is to produce and affirm individuals to experience the abundant living Jesus wants for them.

For some, the apprenticeship to successful single living and discipleship requires a great investment of time and energy. Some singles require affirmation and reaffirmation and support in more generous measures than others.

But by "holding our tongues" we can make a difference.

THE MINISTRY OF MEEKNESS

Too often our verbal emphasis is "WE are God's children," rather than "we are GOD'S children." A simple inflection of the voice makes a big difference. We are not to pride ourselves on what we do not do (smoke/drink/frequent discos/sleep around), but on *whose* we are! When we understand whose we are, we understand who we are.

Part of meekness is being kind to those we do not want to date. Occasionally, halfway through a date we wish we were with someone else. How to end a date is important. We do not have a right to put anyone down.

Nor should we "use" someone just to get us out of the house. How often have you gone out with someone and thought about your date: *You'll do until someone better comes along*? Too many single adults have concluded that a bad date is better than no date.

THE MINISTRY OF LISTENING

We hear with our ears; we listen with our ears, eyes, and hearts. Few single adults listen. But almost all singles are hungry for someone to listen to them. Bonhoeffer concluded, "The *first* service that one owes to others in the fellowship consists of listening to them. Just as to love God begins with listening to His Word, so the beginning of love for another is listening to them."[6]

Singles are so uncomfortable with silence. "Somebody say something!"

Many single adults have ineffective listening habits. We listen for strategic advantage, the break for breath, in which we can seize the conversation and turn it to our interests. We use that phrase "not changing the subject" to change the subject. We cannot permit the pace of the conversation to be controlled or determined by another. We *must* dominate. Psychologist Warren Farrell defined the problem as "self-listening." A single will

> listen to the first sentence or two that a person makes, assume that he knows what is to follow and [start] forming his own story related to his own accomplishments or ego while the other person is still talking. . . . Then, at the first pause, jumping in with his already prepared story . . . he generally drops in a credential and ends his story by a reference to himself, which encourages the group to focus on something he brought up rather than return to the talker.[7]

Singles insert phrases like *I've found* or *It seems to me* or *It has been my experience* and often *If I were you.*

Then we go away thinking we have heard each other. Too often we are so preoccupied or over-occupied with our own world that we fail to hear another. Have you ever had to call someone and ask, "What was it that you told me?"

Some singles listen with their eyes six inches over the speaker's shoulders, especially at parties where contacts need to be made. I had a single friend who attended a large business-related mixer. She told everyone she talked to at the reception, "Today I found out I have cancer."

No one called her hand. Listening is an investment in the life of another. Initial listening lays a foundation for the bigger, more important conversations.

THE MINISTRY OF HELPFULNESS

Many of our great-grandfathers were farmers. They spent time helping neighbors build barns or "pitching in" with the crops or harvest when there was an illness or a special need. That trait will soon have to be exhibited in the Smithsonian.

We are all so busy that "I'd like to help you, but. . ." doesn't even offend people anymore. We *expect* such excuses. Tight, busy schedules are status symbols.

Some only need a moment of our time, a smile, or a word of encouragement. Bonhoeffer, an extremely busy scholar, wrote: "We must be ready to allow ourselves to be interrupted by God. God will be constantly crossing our paths and canceling our plans by sending people with claims and petitions."[8]

Have you learned how to gracefully twist your arm to see your watch without the other person catching you? We have all experienced such gestures as a put-down. So we have had to rearrange our burdens and limp away.

We need to be helpful.

THE MINISTRY OF BEARING

Paul put it simply, "Bear one another's burdens" (Gal. 6:2, NASB). We are a chain, only as strong as the weakest link.

Sometimes the ministry of bearing is inconvenient or unrewarding. We cannot carry another's burdens indefinitely, but we can help repack the load so that it is easier to carry.

One single shares his pain and awareness with another; one beggar tells another where there is shelter from the cold. In an impersonal world we need to make room for others in our lives.

Part of burden-bearing is the need to learn how to share. Particularly feelings. In conferences I have been surprised by the number of women who have said they wished their male friends could open up and share their feelings and emotions. For emotion that is suppressed always erupts or finds a way to announce its presence.

We are so impatient. We want to be today what we can only be tomorrow because of today's experience. Paul assured us that "He who began a good work in you will carry it on to completion until the day of Christ Jesus" (Phil. 1:6). Our personhood ultimately can only be developed through the artistry of Jesus.

I spent a lot of time recently looking at picture frames. I needed just the right frame that would complement the picture without distraction. Circumstances act as "frames" on our lives and personal growth. I am more than the tragedies and experiences—either positive or negative—of my life. God's Word says, "My grace is sufficient for you, for My power is made perfect in weakness" (2 Cor. 12:9). We would like to change that to "perfect in strength" because of "success" thinking. But sometimes we learn more keenly through failures.

The church must provide spiritual and emotional support to the single adult who prayerfully asks, "What can I be or become through His grace?" Some need encouragement and prodding, to honestly confront that question.

The single Christian is capable of living a redemptive fulfilled life: fully single and fully Christian. Paul points to Jesus as "the great example" rather than an unattainable idea. William Phipps suggests reading 1 Corinthians 13 with *Jesus* replacing *love* or *charity*. Then on the second reading insert *I*.

Jesus is patient. . . . Am I patient?
Jesus is kind. . . . Am I kind?
Jesus does not envy or boast. . . . Do I envy or boast?
Jesus is not proud. . . . Am I proud?
Jesus is not rude. . . . Am I rude?
Jesus is not self-seeking. . . . Am I self-seeking?
Jesus is not easily angered. . . . Am I easily angered?
Jesus keeps no record of wrongs. . . . Do I keep a record?
Jesus does not delight in evil. . . . Do I delight in evil?
Jesus rejoices in the truth. . . . Do I rejoice in the truth?
Jesus always protects. . . . Do I always protect?
Jesus always trusts. . . . Do I always trust?
Jesus always hopes. . . . Do I always hope?
Jesus always perseveres. . . . Do I persevere?
Jesus never fails![9]

Only in the mirror of the being of Jesus can a single adult adequately deal with singleness. We must exchange our perceptions (based on the traditions of this world) to assume completeness through the Son of man.

Again, Paul's words urge us to consider our lives. "See to it that no one takes you captive through hollow and deceptive philosophy, which depends on human tradition and the basic principles of this world rather than on Christ" (Col. 2:8-10).

Are you a captive to your singleness?

ONE EXAMPLE

One example of a man who was not captive was Dietrich Bonhoeffer. He declined the safety of a teaching post at Union Seminary in New York. Instead, he chose to return to Nazi Germany to lead opposition to Hitler. He could have been safe and secure. He could have waited out the war and then returned to his homeland. However, he chose a different agenda. "I shall have no right," he decided, "to participate in the reconstruction of Christian life in Germany after the war if I do not share the trials of time with my people."[10]

Bonhoeffer found no time for marriage though he did for love. He stepped up his efforts against Hitler. Earlier, he had organized an illegal, clandestine seminary to train future pastors. He shared a common life and commitment with twenty-five other men. Out of that experience he wrote *Life Together*, a remarkable book on ministry. He wrote that when Christ called a man He bid him come and die.

Then, after his arrest by the Gestapo, prison became a community in which he could practice his ministry. What a laboratory. Many people seek friendship because they are afraid to be alone.

> Because they cannot stand loneliness they are driven to seek the company of other people. There are Christians, too, who cannot endure being alone, who have had some bad experiences with themselves, who hope they will gain some help in association with others. They are generally disappointed. Then they blame the fellowship for what is really their own fault. The Christian community is not a spiritual sanitarium. The person who comes into a fellowship because he is running away from himself is misusing it for the sake of diversion, no matter how spiritual the diversion may appear. He is really not seeking community at all, but only distraction which will allow him time to forget his loneliness for a brief time.[11]

In 1945, Bonhoeffer comforted his fellow prisoners during the intense Allied bombing; his cell was seldom locked. In such circumstances he reflected on the decisions that had brought him to that point—and his approaching execution.

> I often wonder who I really am—the man who goes on squirming under these ghastly experiences in wretchedness or the man who scourges himself and pretends to others (and even to himself) that he is placid, cheerful, composed, and in control of himself, and allows people to admire him for it.

> I *sometimes feel* as if my life were more or less over, as if all I had to do now were to finish my ethics. But you know, *when I feel like this,* there comes over me a longing (unlike any other that I experience) not to vanish without a trace.[12]

Bonhoeffer was hanged by the Nazis. He gave his life to a costly discipleship. He could have cursed his singleness; fought for marriage (and many women would have been willing to be Mrs. Dietrich Bonhoeffer); but he did not.

Ironically, this world will never be the same because of that German single adult. He has not vanished "without a trace." Four decades after his death, he is better known than when he lived. His *Cost of Discipleship* is a classic.

Bonhoeffer could easily have enjoyed New York, married, had children, influenced future scholars and authors, and still be alive and writing—but he heard the Lord's voice and obeyed. This single adult found Christ to be sufficient. He found the bottom to be solid.

CONCLUSION

In the quiet corridors of our hearts, we often recognize the shallowness of our own desires. How ashamed we feel. Bonhoeffer wrote:

> When the Bible speaks of following Jesus, it is proclaiming a discipleship which will liberate mankind from all man-made dogmas, from every burden and oppression, from every anxiety and torture which afflict the conscience. If they follow Jesus, men escape from the hard yoke of their own laws, and submit to the kindly yoke of Jesus.[13]

Jesus says, "My yoke is easy and My burden is light" (Matt. 11:30). Jesus' call is not to be fragile or to live less than a dynamic, fulfilled singleness. If anything it is a call to be more courageous, more disciplined. It is a call to become fully all that God dreams for you to become. To be free to explore the ministry gifts He has given you. To take your place in that long line of single adults, like Bonhoeffer, who chose to be kingdom-seekers—and who made a difference!

EPILOGUE

In the first chapter I asked, *What does it mean to be an adult?* I closed that chapter by asking a second question, *Are you fulfilling God's purpose for your life?* Hopefully, by this point, you have a better understanding of your faith, your singleness, and your adulthood.

I'm reminded of a conversation I had a few years ago with my friend, Ann Kiemel Anderson. At that time we were both single. We discussed our futures. She insisted that I would marry and that she would remain single. That's not the way it turned out. Singleness does have its surprises.

But I have appreciated Ann's book, *I Gave God Time.* Read Ann's words:

i gave God time . . . and room and space.
He worked to create in me, His child,
a more quiet, centered place.
a deeper root of peace and trust.
He never fails to come through.[1]

No doubt many single adults have not read Ann's book. They feel they have given God ample time. But again Ann's words ring true:

Jesus, if this is Your will,
then YES to being single.
in my deepest heart, i want to marry,

to belong to a great man;
to know that i am linked to his life...
and he to mine...
following Christ and our dreams together...
but You know what i need.
if i never marry, it is YES to You.[2]

That's what *Positively Single* is all about. A commitment to seeking FIRST the kingdom of God. Paying more than lip service to Matthew 6:33.

Being positively single is daring to believe that Jesus is who He said He is and that He can enable us to be positive and single throughout this season called singleness.

FOOTNOTES

What Does It Mean to Be an Adult?

[1]U.S. Bureau of the Census, Current Population Reports, Series P-20, No. 389. *Marital Status and Living Arrangements: March 1983* (Washington, D.C.: U.S. Government Printing Office, 1984), p. 1.

[2]Robert J. Havinghurst, *Developmental Tasks and Education,* 3rd ed. (New York: Longman Inc., 1972), pp. 83-94.

[3]*Ibid.*, pp. 95-106.

[4]David Duncombe, *The Shape of the Christian Life* (Nashville: Abingdon Press, 1969), p. 23.

[5]Lawrence J. Crabb, Jr. and Dan B. Allender, *Encouragement: The Key to Caring* (Grand Rapids: Zondervan, 1984), p. 52.

[6]*Ibid.*

[7]Fred Moody, "How Does It Feel to Be Single and Over 30?" *Dallas Observer,* July 11, 1985, p. 1.

[8]Alfred Armand Montapert, *The Supreme Philosophy of Man,* rev. ed. (Los Angeles: Books of Value, 1970), p. 89.

[9]Alan Jones, *Exploring Spiritual Direction* (New York: Seabury Press, 1982), p. 42.

[10]Horatio G. Stafford, "It Is Well with My Soul," *Praise! Our Songs and Hymns* (Grand Rapids: Zondervan, 1979), p. 321.

[11]*The Book of Common Prayer* (New York: Seabury Press, 1979), p. 836.

[12]"A Mother's Crusade Keeps Man in Prison," *Kansas City Times,* June 24, 1985, p. II-1.

[13]Joseph C. Aldrich, *Love For All Your Worth* (Portland: Multnomah Press, 1985), p. 16.

[14]Harold W. Bernard, *Human Development in Western Culture* (Boston: Allyn and Bacon, 1962), p. 383.

Coming to Terms with Yourself

[1]R.T. Williams, lecture, First United Methodist Church, Tulsa, Oklahoma, October 17, 1981.

[2]Karen Tornberg, "Michele Pillar: On Stage for Singles," *Christian Life* (January 1985), p. 34.

[3]Robert Wicks, *The Interpreter's Bible,* Volume XI (Nashville: Abingdon Press, 1980), pp. 124-125.

Coming to Terms with Your Body

[1]David A. Seamands, *Healing for Damaged Emotions* (Wheaton: Victor Books, 1981), pp. 49-54.

[2]Irwin Ross, "Feelings of Inferiority," *Sky* (May 1980),

pp. 70-72.

[3]M. Blaine Smith, *One of a Kind: A Biblical View of Self-Acceptance* (Downers Grove: InterVarsity Press, 1984), p. 48.

[4]*Ibid.*

[5]*Ibid., p. 70.*

[6]Jonathan Edwards, ed., *The Life and Diary of David Brainerd* (Chicago: Moody Press, 1949), p. 120.

[7]*Ibid.,* p. 105.

Coming to Terms with Your Parents

[1]Howard M. Halpern, *Cutting Loose: An Adult Guide to Coming to Terms with Your Parents* (New York: Bantam Books, 1983), pp. 82-91.

[2]Linda Schierse Leonard, *The Wounded Woman: Healing the Father-Daughter Relationship* (Boulder: Shambhala Publications, Inc., 1983), pp. 88-89; 159.

[3]Robert Anderson, *I Never Sang for My Father* in *The Best Plays of 1967-1968* (New York: Dodd, Mead and Co., 1968), p. 281, quoted by Linda Leonard, *The Wounded Woman,* p. 154.

[4]Leonard, *op. cit.,* p. 157.

[5]Leonard Woods, *A Sermon Delivered at the Tabernacle in Salem, February 6, 1812, on the Occasion of the Ordination* (Boston, 1812), p. 32.

[6]Evelyn Wingo Thompson, *Luther Rice: Believer in Tomorrow* (Nashville: Broadman Press, 1967), pp. 201-203.

Coming to Terms with Your Work

[1]Katherine Lackman, *Arkenstone* (March/April 1981), p. 19.

[2]John Bartlett, *Familiar Quotations* (Boston: Little, Brown & Co., 1980), p. 16.

[3]*Ibid.*, p. 572.

[4]Catherine B. Allen, *The New Lottie Moon Story* (Nashville: Broadman Press, 1980), p. 272.

[5]Mary L. Hammack, *A Dictionary of Women in Church History* (Chicago: Moody Press, 1984), p. 10.

[6]Bartlett, *op. cit.*, p. 474.

[7]Marcia Stammell, "Is Your Job Meeting Your Needs?" *Working Woman* (June 1985), pp. 117-119.

Coming to Terms with Your Friends

[1]Art Carey, *In Defense of Marriage* (New York: Walker & Co., 1984), p. 109.

[2]Eugene Kennedy, *Sexual Counseling: A Practical Guide for Non-Professional Counselors* (New York: Continuum Publishing Co., 1977), pp. x-xii.

[3]Barbara Sicherman and Carol Hurd Green, *Notable American Women: The Modern Period: A Biographical Dictionary* (Cambridge: Belknap, 1980), p. xvi; Catherine Clinton, *The Other Civil War: American Women in the Nineteenth Century* (New York: Hill & Wang, Inc., 1984), pp. 137, 163-164.

[4]Herb Goldberg, *The Hazards of Being Male* (New York:

Nash, 1976), p. 142.

[5]Ben Patterson, "Editorial: What Do You Say?" *The Wittenburg Door* (August-September 1983), p. 34.

[6]Sidney Jourard, *The Transparent Self: Self-Disclosure and Well Being* (New York: Van Nostrand Reinhold Co., 1971), p. 5.

[7]*Ibid., p. 59.*

Coming to Terms with Your Anxiety

[1]Dan Kiley, *The Peter Pan Syndrome* (New York: Dodd, Mead & Co., 1983), pp. 86-87.

[2]Mack R. Douglas, *How to Make a Habit of Succeeding* (Grand Rapids: Zondervan, 1966) p. 80.

[3]Frank B. Minirth and Paul D. Meier, *Happiness Is a Choice* (Grand Rapids: Baker Book House, 1978), pp. 168-169.

[4]Jerome Kagan, *The Nature of the Child* (New York: Basic Books, 1984), p. 280.

[5]Frank Stagg, *Broadman Bible Commentary,* vol. 8 (Nashville: Broadman Press, 1969), pp. 118-119.

[6]*Ibid.,* p. 119.

[7]Thomas O. Chisholm, "Great Is Thy Faithfulness," *Praise! Our Songs and Hymns* (Grand Rapids: Zondervan, 1979), p. 54.

[8]Anita Robinson, Isidore Products.

[9]Minirth and Meier, *op. cit.*, pp. 170-171.

[10]Henry C. Thiessen, *Lectures in Systematic Theology*, rev. ed. (Grand Rapids: Eerdmans, 1979), pp. 137-144.

[11]Michael Podesta, Isidore Products.

Coming to Terms with Guilt

[1]Paul Tournier, *Guilt and Grace* (New York: Harper & Row, 1982), p. 136.

[2]Paul Ricoeur in *Guilt and Grace*, p. 190.

[3]Andrew Greeley, *Ascent into Hell* (New York: Warner Books, 1983), p. 492.

[4]Pithy Pottery © by Kathy's Klaythings, Colorado Springs, Colorado.

[5]John Bartlett, *Familiar Quotations* (Boston: Little, Brown & Co., 1980), p. 227.

[6]Dee Brown, *The Gentle Tamers: Women of the Old West* (Lincoln: University of Nebraska, 1958), pp. 243-245.

[7]Frank Bottome, "The Comforter Has Come " (Nazarene Publishing House, 1965).

[8]Doug Manning, *Don't Take My Grief Away* (San Francisco: Harper & Row, 1984), p. 53.

[9]Tournier, *op. cit.*, p. 174.

[10]*Ibid.*

[11]*Ibid.*

Coming to Terms with Resentment

[1]Kenneth O. Gangel, *Leadership for Christian Education* (Chicago: Moody Press, 1972), p. 195.

[2]Fred E. Young, "I and II Samuel," *The Wycliffe Bible Commentary,* ed. by Charles F. Pfeiffer and Everett F. Harrison (Chicago: Moody Press, 1962), p. 299.

[3]Ferdinand Piper, *Lives of Church Leaders or Heroes of the Cross,* trans. Henry Mitchell Maccracken (Cleveland: F.M. Barton, 1879), pp. 114-115; *The Wycliffe Biographical Dictionary of the Church,* ed. Earle E. Cairns (Chicago: Moody Press, 1982), p. 317.

[4]*Ibid.*

Coming to Terms with Jesus

[1]Bruce Larson, *No Longer Strangers* (Waco: Word, 1985), p. 56.

[2]Anita Robertson, calligraphy.

[3]George Gilder, *Naked Nomads* (New York: Times Books, 1974), p. 10 quoted in Barbara Ehrenreich, *The Hearts of Men: American Dreams and the Flight from Commitment* (Garden City: Doubleday, 1984), p. 167.

[4]Urban T. Holmes, III, *Spirituality of Ministry* (San Francisco: Harper & Row, 1983), p. 134.

[5]"Heroes Are Back," *U.S. News and World Report,* 98 (April 22, 1985), pp. 44-45.

[6]Mike Yaconelli, "Thou Shalt Have No Other Celebrities Before Thee," *The Wittenburg Door* (December-January 1983-1984), 31.

[7]*Ibid.*

[8]*Ibid.*

[9]Kathy Doran David, "Charles W. Colson: Confronting Casual Christianity," *The Christian Writer* (July 1984), p. 12.

[10]Bob Benson, address, Nazarene Writer's Conference, Olathe, Kansas, August 22, 1983.

[11]David, *op. cit.*, p. 12.

[12]Gary Collins, "Beyond Easy Believism," presentation Northwest Christian Singles Conference, Tacoma, Washington, March 16, 1984. See also *Beyond Easy Believism* (Waco: Word, 1982).

[13]Wayne E. Oates, *The Struggle to Be Free: My Story and Yours* (Philadelphia: Westminster Press, 1983), p. 47.

[14]Russell Dilday, graduation address, Southern Baptist Seminary, Louisville, Kentucky, May 24, 1985.

[15]Oswald Chambers, *My Utmost for His Highest* (New York: Dodd, Mead & Co., 1935), p. 260.

Coming to Terms with Death

[1]U.S. Bureau of Census, *Statistical Abstract of the United States*, 105th ed. (Washington, D.C.: U.S. Department of Commerce, 1985), pp. 74-79.

[2]Sue and Gail Howard, *I Am Afraid* (Pasadena: World Wide Missions, 1973), p. 72.

[3]M. Scott Peck, *People of the Lie* (New York: Simon and Schuster, 1983), p. 43.

[4]William Sloan Coffin, "Death: More Friend than Foe,"

The Christian Ministry, 16 (May 1985), p. 5.

[5]Frederick Beuchner, *This Sacred Journey* (San Francisco: Harper & Row, 1982), pp. 40-41.

[6]*Ibid.,* p. 48

[7]Jim Geary to Harold Ivan Smith, personal letter March 27, 1984.

[8]Personal correspondence.

[9]*Ibid.*

[10]Colleen Leahy Johnson and Donald J. Catalano, "Childless Elderly and Their Family Supports," *The Gerontologist,* 21 (December 1981), p. 614.

[11]*Ibid.,* p. 616.

[12]*Ibid.*

[13]Matthew Fox, *A Spirituality Called Compassion* (New York: Winston Press, 1978), p. 119.

[14]Daniel W. Steele, "A Boy Thirteen," *Religion and Intellectual Life,* 2 (Spring 1985), p. 57.

[15]Doug Manning, *Don't Take My Grief Away* (San Francisco: Harper & Row, 1984).

[16]*Ibid.*

[17]Mary Christine DeBardeleben, *Lambuth-Bennett Book of Rememberance* (Nashville: Publishing House of Methodist Episcopal Church, South, 1922), p. 113.

[18]"The Founding of Moody Institute," *Moody Monthly*

(February 1985), p. 32.

[19]*The Book of Common Prayer* (New York: Seabury Press, 1979), p. 862.

[20]Coffin, *op. cit.,* p. 6.

[21]Howard, *op. cit.,* p. 25.

[22]Norbert Elias, *The Loneliness of Dying* (London: Basil Blackwell, Ltd., 1985), p. 3.

[23]Howard, *op. cit.,* back cover.

Coming to Terms with Ministry

[1]Dietrich Bonhoeffer, *Life Together,* trans. by John W. Doberskin (New York: Harper & Row, 1945), p. 23.

[2]*Ibid.,* p. 106.

[3]Jason Towner, "I Am Alone," *Warm Reflections* (Nashville: Broadman Press, 1977), p. 15.

[4]Bonhoeffer, *op. cit.,* p. 97.

[5]Gabrielle Brown, *The New Celibacy* (New York: McGraw-Hill, 1980).

[6]Bonhoeffer, *op. cit.,* p. 97.

[7]Warren Farrell, *The Liberated Man, Beyond Masculinity* (New York: Random House, 1975), p. 11.

[8]Bonhoeffer, *op. cit.,* p. 99.

[9]William E. Phipps, *The Sexuality of Jesus; Theological and Literary Perspectives* (New York: Harper & Row, 1973), p. 140.

[10]Dietrich Bonhoeffer, *The Cost of Discipleship,* rev. ed. (New York: Macmillan, 1968), p. 16.

[11]J. Martin Bailey and Douglas Gilbert, *The Steps of Bonhoeffer* (Philadelphia: Pilgrim, n.d.), p. 55.

[12]*Ibid.,* p. 77.

[13]*Ibid.,* p. 50.

Epilogue

[1]Ann Kiemel Anderson, *I Gave God Time* (Wheaton: Tyndale, 1982), p. 20.

[2]*Ibid.*

RECOMMENDED READING

One of the gifts I have most appreciated across the years is the recommendation of a good book. I'd like to share some suggestions for those of you who would like to further explore the topics covered in this book.

WHAT DOES IT MEAN TO BE AN ADULT?

Joseph C. Aldrich, *Love for All Your Worth,* Multnomah Press, 1985.

Alan Jones, *Exploring Spiritual Direction,* Seabury Press, 1982.

COMING TO TERMS WITH YOURSELF

David A. Seamands, *Putting Away Childish Things,* Victor Books, 1982.

COMING TO TERMS WITH YOUR BODY

David A. Seamands, *Healing for Damaged Emotions,* Victor Books, 1981.

M. Blaine Smith, *One of a Kind: A Biblical View of Self-Acceptance,* InterVarsity Press, 1984.

COMING TO TERMS WITH YOUR PARENTS

Elva McAllaster, *When a Father Is Hard to Honor,* Brethren Press, 1984.

COMING TO TERMS WITH YOUR WORK

Denis Waitley & Reni L. Witt, *The Joy of Working,* Dodd, Mead & Co., 1985.

COMING TO TERMS WITH YOUR FRIENDS

Alan Loy McGinnis, *The Friendship Factor,* Augsburg Publishing House, 1979.

Alan Loy McGinnis, *Bringing Out the Best in People,* Augsburg Publishing House, 1985.

COMING TO TERMS WITH YOUR ANXIETY

Frank R. Minirth and Paul D. Meier, *Happiness Is a Choice,* Baker Book House, 1978.

COMING TO TERMS WITH GUILT

Jason Towner, *Forgiveness Is for Giving,* Zondervan Publishing House, 1984.

COMING TO TERMS WITH RESENTMENT

Richard J. Foster, *Freedom of Simplicity,* Harper & Row, 1981.

Richard J. Foster, *Money, Sex, & Power,* Harper & Row, 1985.

COMING TO TERMS WITH JESUS

Gary Collins, *Beyond Easy Believism,* Word Inc., 1982.

Oswald Chambers, *My Utmost for His Highest,* Dodd, Mead, & Co., 1935.

Bruce Larson, *No Longer Strangers,* Word Inc., 1985.

Wayne Oates, *The Struggle to Be Free,* Westminster Press, 1983.

COMING TO TERMS WITH DEATH

Doug Manning, *Don't Take My Grief Away,* Harper & Row, 1984.

COMING TO TERMS WITH MINISTRY

Dietrich Bonhoeffer, *Life Together,* translated by John W. Doberstein, Harper & Row, 1945.

Dietrich Bonhoeffer, *The Cost of Discipleship,* revised edition, Harper & Row, 1968.

Jeanne Doering, *The Power of Encouragement,* Moody Press, 1983.

Urban T. Holmes, *Spirituality for Ministry,* Harper & Row, 1982.

Harold Ivan Smith, *Tear-Catchers: Developing the Gift of Compassion,* Abingdon Press, 1984.